1001

andy kirkpatrick

CLIMBING TIPS

MOUNTAINEERS
BOOKS

1001 CLIMBING TIPS

andy kirkpatrick

MOUNTAINEERS BOOKS

Mountaineers Books is the publishing division of The Mountaineers, an organization founded in 1906 and dedicated to the exploration, preservation, and enjoyment of outdoor and wilderness areas.

1001 SW Klickitat Way, Suite 201, Seattle, WA 98134
800.553.4453, www.mountaineersbooks.org

This Work was originally published in 2016 by Vertebrate Publishing, an imprint of Vertebrate Graphics Ltd, Crescent House, 228 Psalter Lane, Sheffield, S11 8UT, UK, under the title *1001 Climbing Tips* by Andy Kirkpatrick.

Printed in Korea

20 19 18 17   1 2 3 4 5

Design and layout: Nathan Ryder
Photography Andy Kirkpatrick Collection unless otherwise credited
Original illustrations by Andy Kirkpatrick
Front cover photograph: *Creative cam placement on a solo ascent of* Sea of Dreams, *El Cap*

Library of Congress Cataloging-in-Publication Data

Names: Kirkpatrick, Andy, 1971- author.
Title: 1001 climbing tips / Andy Kirkpatrick.
Other titles: One thousand one climbing tips
Description: Seattle, Washington : Mountaineers Books, [2017] | "This Work was originally published in 2016 by Vertebrate Publishing, an imprint of Vertebrate Graphics Ltd, Crescent House, 228 Psalter Lane, Sheffield, S11 8UT, UK, under the title 1001 Climbing Tips by Andy Kirkpatrick"--T.p. verso. | Includes bibliographical references.
Identifiers: LCCN 2017016887 | ISBN 9781680511314 (paperback)
Subjects: LCSH: Mountaineering--Handbooks, manuals, etc. | Rock climbing--Handbooks, manuals, etc.
Classification: LCC GV200 .K567 2017 | DDC 796.522--dc23 LC record available at https://lccn.loc.gov/2017016887

ISBN (paperback): 978-1-68051-131-4

"Never listen to any advice, including this."
ANDY KIRKPATRICK – HULL'S SECOND BEST CLIMBER

warning
climbing is dangerous

ENTHUSIASM IS NO SUBSTITUTE
FOR EXPERIENCE

This manual is designed to give climbers the skills necessary to
stay safe, but rock climbing and mountaineering are inherently
dangerous and so this manual is written for experienced rock
climbers and mountaineers only. No one should undertake
climbing without the proper training or equipment, and
individuals must take personal responsibility for learning the
proper techniques and employing good judgement. I strongly
recommend that anyone who is unsure about any aspect of
this manual seeks instruction from a qualified professional.
By using the information contained within this manual you
acknowledge that the information herein may be out of date
or inaccurate and you agree that the author, publisher or rights
holder cannot be held responsible or liable for any damage or
injury that may be caused as a result of using this manual.

cont

ents

introdu

It's often said by writers of books like this that they would have loved to have had a copy when they had been novices, as having one would have avoided all those silly mistakes you make when you're starting out. Although when I was a novice I read everything I could, and absorbed every crumb of information I could lay my hands on, I'd disagree with that. Discovering these things, these 1,001 tips, was part of what made me a climber, and it's really the learning that's important, not so much what you learn.

What you learn is the easy part.

Climbing is a simple sport and, given long enough, most people can work out for themselves how to do anything: from climbing up a blank boulder, to scaling a mile-high wall – it's the buzz of working it out that makes climbing so addictive. This is why climbing has such a rich history of photographers, poets, writers and filmmakers, as well as thinkers and tinkerers of technique – it attracts people who like to think.

I was lucky in that my dad was a climbing instructor in the Royal Air Force; working for most of his career in the mountain rescue he had made a career out of teaching people to climb. Along the way he seemed to have struck on the idea that you need to give people the ability to learn for themselves – quite a bold move when your job is to teach – as that way the student can be their own instructor. I guess it's a bit like the old adage, 'If you give a man a fish he can eat for a day, but if you teach him to fish he can feed himself for life'. That's what my dad did for me, he taught me to fish. Little things like, 'how do you make a harness out of tape?', or 'how do you make a death slide?', would just lead to him giving me a book, or just giving me the most basic of instructions. At the time I used to get very frustrated and would want him to just tell me, or better still just tie the bloody knot or set up the death slide. Having to work it out led to all sorts of mistakes, big and small, but I lived through them and learnt the hard way.

Years later, having devoured everything I could about climbing, I began to move on to areas of climbing where there was no available knowledge, neither written down or locked away in the head of someone whom I could ask. Wanting to solo El Cap for the first time, or speed climbing as a three-person team, was an exercise of simply working through the process backwards, sort of reverse engineering a problem. Often this learning, such as how to tag gear on lead (hanging it from a fifi hook) so I didn't have to carry all the rack, had to be worked out while on lead, while other things such as how to deal with stuck haul bags were worked out in a quarry near my house (you have a wall hauler on the bag). And so many times I've looked back at my early days of learning and thanked my dad, not for what he taught me, but for what he didn't.

ction

So why write a book with a thousand tips in it? Well I guess there was that challenge to begin with: seeing if I could think of that many tips. Could I suck all my knowledge out of my head and fit it into a book? And then as a climbing instructor I also tend not to practise what I preach all the time, and although I think that working it out for yourself is best, I love helping people hotwire their experience. I also recognise that passing on knowledge and not locking it away is a part of most sports, and is what allows a sport to develop; the next generation getting a head start on the last, all that 'standing on people's shoulders' stuff.

There are no earth-shattering tips in this book, no Mongolian levitation chants or Tibetan rock-shoe rubber resole spells; just simple nuggets about all aspects of climbing (some gold, some just rolled gold). This is not an instruction book – it presumes that you already know quite a bit about climbing – and a novice will probably grow to understand the relevance of some tips as they progress. Others will find some tips either wrong, rubbish or just plain stupid. I must point out that this book is not inclusive, and is simply about stuff that works for me but may not work for others.

Think of this book as a thousand little bits of advice passed on at the crag, down the wall or in the pub; those little things that can make a tiny, or massive, improvement to your climbing. I'm sure that even with so many bits of experience, you'll still learn most of what you need to learn anyway, and more importantly you'll make just as many fabulous mistakes.

Here's to mistakes.

acknowledgments

Apart from my dad, who taught me how to work it out for myself, I owe a lot to my old boss Dick Turnbull, who was always willing – often too willing – to share his experience. Dick had climbed the north faces of the Eiger, Matterhorn and Grandes Jorasses, and this coloured his thinking on gear and technique – basically Dick was a survivor. At the same time, even though he knew so much, he was never so dogmatic as not to listen and learn from others. His article on winter Alpine climbing in *High* magazine back in the 1990s kick-started my interest in writing about gear, and my masochistic obsession with winter Alpine climbing. (Good gear gives the impression of suffering while actually being relatively comfy … relatively.)

I also need to thank my many partners who took gear and technique seriously and were always looking at new ways of improving both: people like Rich Cross, Paul Ramsden, Al Powell and Rolando Garibotti typify this approach. I should also add the partners who took no interest in either, like Ian Parnell, Matt Dickinson and Paul Tattersall – they showed me that just being good was good enough.

One group that would be easy to overlook would be crags such as Stanage and Millstone Edge in Derbyshire, which, although less than a rope-length high, taught me all I needed to know in order to attempt big walls and faces further afield. And those faces and walls, such as the Troll Wall, El Cap and the Dru, that taught me the hard lessons I needed to survive.

Lastly, thanks to Aggelos Orfanakos for spending many hours climbing a mountain of typos!

notes

UNIT CONVERSION

The following data may help you convert the units discussed in the text.

1 kilometre	=	0.62 miles
1 metre	=	1.09 yards or 3.28 feet
1 centimetre	=	0.39 inches
1 kilogram	=	2.2 pounds (lbs)
1 litre	=	2.11 pints

FEEDBACK AND UPDATES

If you have any feedback or questions regarding this book, perhaps where more clarity is needed (like a diagram), then please drop me a line: *andy@psychovertical.com*

My website also has a ton of articles on technique, skills and assorted climbing obsessiveness: *www.andy-kirkpatrick.com*

CLIMBING TERMS

Throughout this guidebook, I obviously use British climbing terms, most of which are also familiar in North America. Two, however, are not:

lark's foot = girth hitch
peg = piton

this book sucks

Have you ever seen the film *Starship Troopers* by the hugely misunderstood Danish director Paul Verhoeven? He is the director responsible for such classics as *Robocop*, *Total Recall*, *Basic Instinct* and *Showgirls*, so is in a class all by himself.

In the film, which is about a war between humans and the 'bugs', the giant insect aliens capture two of the heroes, and instead of being cut to bloody pieces like everyone else, they are dragged down into an underground lair. Once there, the 'super brain' alien rocks up and sticks a straw-like

proboscis into one of the heroes' heads and proceeds to suck his brains out, in the process capturing all his thoughts, ideas and memories.

So what's my point? Well, reading this book is a little bit like that – you are now that super alien, and it's my brains that you're about to suck out.

Bon appétit!

Vanessa Sumner on *Crescent Arch*, Daff Dome, Tuolumne Meadows.

The author bushwhacking to the Troll Wall, Norway.

001

BASICS (1–240)

*"A week of good instruction is worth
a year of getting it wrong."*

LEARNING (1–10)

1. There are five basic ways of learning: verbal, visual, tactile, kinaesthetic and aural. From this list, most people will have one or two main ways of learning. I'm a great reader and will read everything I can find on a subject when I get into it, from sea kayaking to writing CSS code, but I'll need to quickly put it into practice (kinaesthetic) for it to take hold. I'll often get my knowledge about 70 per cent there, then start putting it into practice to get the rest. Many of the climbing skills I needed to learn early on had yet to be written up in books, and this was before the web, so using a kinaesthetic and tactile approach I just had to work it out for myself – such as how to solo a big wall. I'm a big believer in 'learning by doing', but everyone is different, something I've learned by climbing with other climbers, and so it's worth working out how you learn best before you set out on the wonderful world of climbing knowledge; knowledge that you will need to get you down from a 5-metre boulder or through to the summit of Everest.

2. A very important thing to know before you set out on amassing climbing knowledge is that although there is a lot of it (just look how big this book is – and this is just the tips!), nearly everything is very, very simple. A rope has two ends. Gravity is always the same: what goes up comes down (eventually). Gear doesn't break: people break gear. So don't get too stressed out about getting it right, and if in doubt just think it through with a rational mind – you'll probably be right.

3. If you want to learn from scratch you'll either need someone to teach you, or you'll need to teach yourself. You can be taught as a climbing apprentice, or as a climbing client; meaning you either need to find a mate or climbing club that will take you under their wing, or you can pay someone to teach you. A mate is an ideal way to learn as you will already have a relationship, while a club can feel closed and cliquish at first, but once settled in you'll be able to tap into a great deal of knowledge. If you go on courses, try out single-day courses first and go with companies or organisations that have a good reputation. Self-teaching through books, the web and DVDs is a good way to build up your knowledge base, but ultimately you're going to need a climbing partner.

4. Getting a partner can be tough, and you can either try and meet someone experienced through an internet forum, climbing club or via someone else (for example, 'my mate Bill goes climbing'), or even through a climbing course close to home. (Climbing walls often run conversion courses for those who want to climb outside, and here you can meet like-minded climbers.) The other way is to teach yourself how to do it, and find a novice who wants to join you.

5. A week of good instruction is worth a year of getting it wrong.

6. Whenever you're climbing with someone you don't know, don't leave your brain on the ground: be super paranoid, as there are many people who brag, bullshit and play the hero in the world of climbing. Don't blindly trust anyone until they have proved themselves trustworthy. Check out if they can tie on, how old their gear is, if they do things that just seem odd. If you don't trust someone, or get a bad feeling, then don't climb with them.

7. Treat climbing skills as you would any other sport, and slowly work through the skills, learning as much as you can as best you can. This means little things like having a length of cord and practising every knot in Nigel Shepherd's *Complete Guide to Rope Techniques* while sitting at home, or going down to the park and practising prusiking and rescue techniques.

8. If you want to get to grips with the basics of belays then do your SPA (Single Pitch Award, per the UK's Mountain Training Association), as the training, logging of climbs and other certificate requirements are good ways to raise your skill level.

9. Slowly building up qualifications via training courses with the associated need to get 'hours in' can build up experience, with the Summer Mountain Leader (Summer ML) and Winter Mountain Leader (Winter ML) being popular courses, also overseen by the Mountain Training Association.

10. The one thing I would say against these courses is that very often it is the search for knowledge on *your own*, and recognition of what *you* are looking for, that is part of the journey. For example, a few people have asked if I can teach them to solo a big wall, to which I reply that learning to solo a big wall yourself is probably the most important skill you can learn in preparation for soloing a big wall. When you're all alone and something has gone wrong, being able to work out what to do on the fly is a vital skill.

PARTNERSHIPS (11–22)

11. It's important that you and your partner are well balanced in experience and ability, but perhaps it is even more important that you share the same degree of psych for the same kinds of climbs: meaning that while one person may outrank the other in ability, what they lack in skill they make up in enthusiasm for hard climbs — even if that's just belaying.

12. If trying out potential partners, go down to the climbing wall first and then progress up to a day at the crag, then a weekend of multi-pitch climbing, and then a longer trip. Just going on a 'blind date' on a major route can work, but it's risky and can be dangerous.

13. If you're looking for an alpine or expedition partner, check how fast they are at completing everyday tasks, like getting geared up, putting their kit away or stuffing a sleeping bag. If they are much slower than you, this can cause problems when you've got to do this in extreme environments. I know of at least one climber who got frostbite while waiting for a slow partner to get sorted.

14. A sense of humour is vital in any partnership, as this will allow you to deal more effectively with setbacks.

15. The psych of a team of two will rise and fall as they climb, with one person at the sharp end one minute, then on belay duty the next. Generally when you're belaying and it's hard, your psych begins to drop, while the leader's psych rises as they progress. Add in darkness, bad weather, route finding errors, dehydration, and so on, and this is compounded. As in warfare, speed is the key, and by moving fast you reduce the chances of either climber's psych reaching rock-bottom. Even then, it takes both climbers' psych levels to fall for a retreat to be called, which will come when both climbers have stopped moving. Basically, the faster you're moving, the slower you'll fail due to a lack of psych.

BASICS (1-240)

16. Like a long marriage, being with the same partner for a long time has its ups and downs, and being a little bit promiscuous can be a good thing. Learning new ideas from new partners, as well as shaking things up, makes climbing more exciting.

17. Having an established partnership allows you to develop a strong bond of understanding between each other, primarily based around crag communication. If you trust your partner you know that when the rope comes tight you're on belay and you can climb, or that when they shout 'take' they aren't asking you to 'take them off.' (This happened to someone I know.) This level of understanding is part of the fellowship of the rope, and is taken for granted until you climb with someone new and nothing is simple.

18. A good partnership is probably one where each climber leapfrogs the other as they progress through the grades. Maybe this is due to some level of competition, but whatever the reason it will help to keep the climbing fresh.

19. Don't be too dogmatic about swinging leads, and if the route is important (i.e. you want to get up it) then put the best climber forward for the pitch they're best suited to. If someone's good at cracks then they can have those pitches. If someone is better at slabs then let them lead. At the same time, don't put yourself in a climbing ghetto where 'you're good at slabs but rubbish at roofs' – aim to be a great all-round climber. But when it comes to simply 'getting up a route' put the best climber in front.

20. If you climb with someone new, and they haven't been vouched for by someone you trust, then treat them as a novice. I've climbed with people who told me they had climbed a lot and who then couldn't tie on, even people who didn't know how to belay, or belayed me on a GriGri only to tell me afterwards they'd never used one before. I've climbed a lot of routes with people who had no right to be there (on paper at least), but who performed well. The difference was I treated them with a great deal of suspicion, and wasn't afraid to ask them dumb questions like 'can you tie on?'

21. If your partnership is going to be tested (say on an alpine trip or expedition) then make sure you put it under as much pressure as possible beforehand, meaning hardcore training trips. See how long or hard you can go before you break. Undertake stupid challenges that will push you without sleep, with reduced food, and with just sheer fatigue, and then see how you cope as a team. If you train harder than you'll ever climb, then you'll find the climbing the easy part.

22. When doing committing routes, try and achieve balance in your preparedness, meaning such things as both of you having rescue insurance, the same amount of food and water, and most of all the willingness to give it everything.

ROPES (23–46)

23. In the good old days climbers were rubbish and never fell off. Now we're ace and fall off all the time; that's why we now have stuff like harnesses, and ropes that don't break. One thing that remains from those heady days when people travelled to crags without airbags or seat belts, or on motorbikes without helmets (while smoking strong cigarettes), is a blasé attitude to safety. It's taken us a couple of decades for people without beards to wear helmets, and tying in is still treated with far too much disrespect. Remember that when 'tying in' you're tying the most important knot of your life.

24. When tying in, treat your partner like a complete idiot, and check they have tied in properly. This is the approach used in skydiving and scuba diving, so why not climbing? Also tell them to treat you as a fool too, although saying so will mean you're not.

25. Get into the habit of not talking when people are tying in. When you're tying what is potentially the most important knot of your life it's best to give it your undivided attention.

26. If you think this is overreacting I suggest you have a search online for what someone's legs look like when they've fallen from 20 or 30 metres, and just think about that each time you tie in, or check your mate's tying in – it really helps to focus the mind.

27. To get the right length of rope for a figure-of-eight knot, just measure the rope from your sternum to your fingertips (for an adult). Keep the knot tight to your harness, so that when you reach down to pull up the rope to clip, you're not grabbing the knot.

28. When tying a figure-of-eight knot (the only knot any self-respecting climber should use to tie in), tie a fisherman's knot (stopper knot) to finish. This has no bearing on safety in itself if you've tied your figure-of-eight knot correctly, but it means that a) you've left enough tail to mean the figure-of-eight knot won't fail due to too short a tail slipping into the knot, and b) if you've failed to finish the figure-of-eight knot then a well-tied fisherman's should keep you alive long enough to realise you're an idiot who should have stuck to golf.

29. There are many times when you should ignore what the harness company said in their instruction booklet about your harness (you did read it, right?), and do the thing that every climbing book and instructor would see as tantamount to doing a Riverdance jig on your new rope. This heresy is to tie directly in to your belay loop! In reality, when wearing loads of clothes, or with frozen hands (or broken fingers), in the dark, then tying in normally is just plain dangerous. Instead, if you don't think you can thread your rope properly, then just tie in to your belay loop, or easier still, tie a figure-of-eight and clip in with two screwgates (or two plain gates back-to-back if you don't have a screwgate). Don't make a habit of it, but also don't let dogma make an already dangerous situation worse (tying on in the rain, in the dark, with frozen fingers that are also broken!).

30. Climbers can belay from their belay loop, from the loop of rope formed when they tie in, or directly from the belay (using a guide plate or Munter hitch – also known as an Italian hitch). Personally, I only belay from my belay loop when belaying the leader, and direct when belaying the second(s) – unless it's not appropriate, and instead I go for a trad belay from my belay loop. I personally never belay from my rope, as I have the nasty habit of forgetting the belay device is attached to the rope, and so when I untie I drop it (the art of being a good climber is to avoid such 'Oh shit' moments).

31. The sheath of a rope provides 20 to 30 per cent of a rope's strength, so if it becomes damaged or worn it's not quite as serious as it may seem. If you're committed, then try and patch the damage with tape (finger tape, duct tape etc.) to reduce wear, but try and avoid abseiling on the rope as this will stress the sheath and may cause it to separate. Once you have a fully broken sheath the core will spill out, making belaying very problematical, and the rope will need to be retired or cut down. (See tip 268 for abseiling on damaged ropes, page 60.)

32. The ends of ropes have a stiff plastic marker heat-shrunk on to them to help identify them, telling you rope length and diameter – great for group use. If they are your ropes then consider cutting these off and melting the end into a lower-profile shape, as this end can often get caught in cracks when rapping. To do this cut off the tip, then pull an inch of core out and cut this off at a steep angle, so the core strands taper, then pull the sheath back over and melt. This should create a more tapered rope end.

33. When you get a new rope always uncoil it carefully with one person holding it while a second unwraps it – ideally into a rope bag. If you just dump it on the floor then it will get kinks and tangles in it that will take time to remove.

34. Rope bags are the only way to go for doing lots of routes in a session, be it at the wall or on the outcrops. There are many great bags out there, but you can make do with something like a heavy-duty IKEA bag, or even just a plastic tarp.

The author on the Lafaille route, Petit Dru. **Photo**: Ian Parnell

35. Try and take pride in having a good tidy system for your ropes when climbing, especially on multi-pitch routes. Always loop them over your belay, and never just let them hang below in some massive tanglefest. When looping, either just loop over your belay, or pass them through a sling. These techniques are ideal if you're climbing in blocks (one person leads a bunch of pitches at a time).

36. When making loops of rope try and make each loop a little shorter than the one before. This means that as you pay the rope(s) out, the loops won't snag into each other.

37. If you're climbing in blocks there is always the problem that the ropes are coiled upside down, and doubly so if you're climbing as a group of three. Some people flip the ropes over, but I think it's just easier to untie and retie in to the correct ends. To do this you'll need to be connected to the belay with a sling or daisy chain.

38. Whenever you use a single rope on any climb you should either tie a knot in the end, or tie in to the end. Many climbers have died or had serious accidents when the rope end has slipped through a device. Even if a route is twenty metres long and you have a 60-metre rope (did you check with your partner that his rope is in fact 60 metres, or did he cut it down as it was worn?), by belaying away from the wall, or walking downhill a short way for a better view, you can soon run out of rope.

39. You can store a rope in three main ways: an alpine coil, a butterfly coil or loose. The alpine coil is less used now, but has some good points. This style is simply the classic round and round coiling of the rope (from neck to waist). This classic shape can be thrown over the shoulder and easily uncoiled in a small space, and it also tends to sit better in a rucksack. One way to carry such a coil is to simply pop it around the lid of your sack, using the lid compression or upper side straps to secure it. The butterfly coil is fast and easy and tends to put fewer twists into the rope, and is the most popular system of stowing a rope. Loose is by far the best way to store a rope, and this can be in a rope bag or bucket.

40. To carry a butterfly coiled rope on your back, just make sure the tails are around 3 metres long, throw the rope over your back, cross the tails over your chest and then around your waist and tie together. By crossing the ropes over your chest to form an 'X' you remove the annoying habit of the rope slipping off your shoulders.

41. When buying ropes try and make sure the colours are strikingly different, ideally so much so that you could even tell them apart in the dark.

42. If you're buying ropes, unless it's for something special, like a particular route or trip which needs something out of the ordinary, then go for robust rope diameters, namely 10.5-millimetre single ropes and 8.5-millimetre half ropes. The norm is 60 metres, so go long.

43. If you climb primarily on short routes under 20 metres but you need double ropes, then you can just buy a single half-rope and double this up. This means you'll not wear two ropes out, only one.

44. If you're on overhanging terrain, avoid dropping the end of your rope if it will fall its full length (so a 60-metre rope's end will drop 60 metres). If you do you'll find that although it makes a cool 'whiplash' sound, the end of the rope will break apart, caused by the end going supersonic, plus if it hits someone below, it could do them some major damage.

45. The two most destructive things you can do to a rope are top roping and jumaring – that is if you're a fool! Always extend a top-rope anchor over an edge, and don't bounce and struggle when jumaring. Both of these will cause the rope to rub and abrade – and if you're unlucky it may even snap.

46. When setting up top ropes it's best to forget about messing around with slings and cordelettes; instead go for a mega cordelette made from 20 metres of thick rope, 9.5-millimetre to 11-millimetre in diameter, static or dynamic. With this you can tame even the most complex of anchors.

Vanessa Sumner on *On the Lamb*, Lamb Dome, Tuolumne Meadows.

PASSIVE PROTECTION (47-83)

47. Passive protection is any protection without any moving parts, so it's the best gear to start out with as it's cheap, strong and easy to understand.

48. If you're climbing with more than one set of nuts, then split them over three karabiners, with one for large nuts (sizes 10 to 7), one for medium nuts (6 to 4), and one for small nuts and micro-wires (3 to 00).

49. I prefer using oval karabiners (Black Diamond wiregate ovals) for racking wires, as the large bottom radius stops the wires bunching up, plus they are a little larger than D-shaped karabiners. Mark the nose of the karabiner with enamel paint so it's easier to identify. (Most of it will come off, but enough will remain to make it easier to identify the nose.)

50. If you split your nuts over different sizes, then you can use different coloured karabiners or spray them. While you're at it, also spray the nuts for each karabiner, so they can be quickly racked at changeovers on to the correct 'biner.

51. It's best to rack your wires on the front portion of your harness, with the small ones at the front and the larger ones at the back (so small krab, medium krab, large krab). This makes it easier to locate the correct nut. The only time I would avoid this is when using a harness with gear loops that are too far forward, which would mean the nuts would always be flopping between your legs and the rope.

52. If you're climbing on granite, sandstone or gritstone then wires are used much less and so they can go further back on the harness, with cams replacing them in your prime harness real estate.

53. Don't think that only the second needs a nut tool, as the leader will often need one as well; they may get nuts stuck while trying to get the right one to fit (stuck, but not in a good way!).

54. Some climbers like to use karabiners with a smooth nose to rack nuts, allowing nuts to slip off easily. Personally I find that they slide off a bit too easily, and you can easily drop quite a few nuts this way. (There is nothing more distressing than watching your nuts falling away between your feet.)

55. If wires get bent at the head then just bend them back into shape. Beware of micro-wires with super-thin cables though, as their strength is very low and repeated bending will damage them. Replace them if any wires are broken. If you do have a broken wire, they are guaranteed to stick into your fingertips just under your nail. (This is God's way to remind you to not be a cheapskate and to replace them.)

56. If you find you need some extra reach, then push the wires through a medium-size nut, and then thread the nut you want to use through this, giving you an extra few inches. I once met someone who thought this was cheating, but then he also thought it was cheating to use any wire, believing you had to put the nut in using your fingers. Looking back, I think he just liked playing devil's advocate.

57. If your nut becomes stuck, try pushing the cable through the head of the nut, attach a draw to this and then yank upwards.

58. A nut tool is a vital item on a climber's rack. It can be used to remove a nut and also to place one, allowing you to tap it into position. Nut tools with a solid head are a little easier to hit with your hand (or head), but they can be harder to slip deep into cracks. There are also some routes where a nut tool is used for gear, but this is generally just a way of scaring newbies, and there is usually a bomber nut placement next to it.

59. On loose and adventurous routes, you often find that there are very good nut placements that are blocked by dirt or tiny stones and pebbles. Digging away with a nut tool will often pay dividends, but having a hammer with a sharp pick is best, as you can blast jammed stones and dirt out of cracks. Some people might call this chipping, but I call it rock gardening or 'gravity's little helper'.

60. A nut tool can easily be dropped and so it's worth attaching a loop of cord to the top of the tool. This can be clipped into the rope when you're seconding if you come across a stubborn piece, or directly into the piece so that it's not dropped when it finally comes loose.

61. When climbing a route you may come across a fixed nut. Always check that it is in fact stuck, and not just balanced there, as it may simply have been forgotten by the last second and simply be junk. On two occasions I've gone to clip fixed 'thank God' nuts only for them to just fall out as soon as I clipped in my rope. On one occasion there was only the wire – and no nut!

62. Also check that fixed nuts aren't corroded, as rusty cables can break under bodyweight. If in doubt, thread a thin sling around the nut, as the nut should be bomber as the aluminium alloy it is made from corrodes more slowly than the steel cable.

63. Another good reason for marking your wires is that it helps you distinguish them from fixed nuts. When the second comes across a nut that is unmarked, they know it's not one of yours and they can just leave it if you're in a hurry.

64. If you run out of extenders on a route then don't forget that you can simply use wires instead. I ideally clip them like extenders (karabiner in each end), but as a last resort (say you're running out of karabiners) then just lark's-foot it through the wire you want to clip (not through the tape of a cam though).

65. Micro-wires with super-thin cables are inherently weak, but they will hold a fall without breaking with stretchy ropes and medium-weight climbers. If you understand fall factors and the physics of climbing, then a heavy climber taking a fall on a single rope close to the belay can break a wire. In these situations double up on the wires if you can (micro-wires side by side), use a screamer sling, or give a dynamic belay to give the wires a fighting chance. Better still; don't fall off on wires as thick as a guitar string.

66. A nut can be placed in many different ways, and simply rotating a nut from one face to another can be the difference between a bomber placement and a crap one. Remember that you're aiming for a stable three-point contact between nut and rock. This will usually be two points on the concave face, and one on the convex face. I once met a man who, when asked what gear you needed for the Eiger North Face, replied, 'a Rock 7', and then proceeded to say how it could be placed once on every pitch, just by rotating it four different ways (I guess you'd take spares though).

BASICS (1-240)

67. The simpler the nut the easier it is for the second to clean, as it has fewer angles to cause problems; Wild Country Rocks and Black Diamond Stoppers are therefore great for beginners. But the more complex shapes found on DMM Wallnuts and Metolius Ultralights give you more options when it comes to difficult placements. When it comes to choosing what to use it's best to have a mix: say one set of simple, one set of complex – plus throw in some offsets (DMM Peenuts and Offset nuts).

68. The best nuts ever made were the now long-dead first generation prototype Wild Country Super Rocks, which went in many places no other nut would. The problem was they were so good they never came out again. The art of a good nut placement is that it provides all the protection a leader may need in a fall, but it can still be easily cleaned by the second without wasting time or energy.

69. If you have trouble finding the right nut to fit the crack, then use your fingers as a guide; work out what size is the same as your fingertip, second knuckle and thumb width. This way you should be able to find the nut that fits more quickly.

70. If you're only carrying one set of nuts, then consider racking them odds and evens on two 'biners (so 1, 3, 5, 7, 9 on one and 2, 4, 6, 8, 10 on the other), this way if you fumble and drop your nuts, you won't lose them all.

71. When weight is an issue, check if you can replace the larger, heavier nuts with hexes, as these may be lighter and offer more range.

72. Big hexes (my generic term for all large alloy nuts such as Rockcentrics or Torque Nuts) are great for winter climbing, where wide cracks may be encountered. One problem with these nuts is that they are hard to place high above the head, as the sling just flops over. To overcome this you can thread some plastic tubing (found in DIY stores) over the sling, making it semi-stiff. Remember to slip it off when you get home so the sling can dry properly.

73. Hexes, due to their shape and flexible sling, allow a great deal of creativity in placement, and they can be placed both as a nut (but with more options due to their shape) or as a camming nut like a Tricam. To cam a hex you need the hex to be pulled into a camming position by the sling (if you play around with Tricams you'll understand this concept more). The DMM Torque Nut is especially good at this. You can also put a hex in 'backwards' so the sling is facing into the rock, then flip it back over the hex, meaning when the sling is pulled, the hex cams backwards. The strength of such a marginal placement is dependent on the intersection of the sling and the hex, as a hard fall may cause the hex to cut the sling, and so it should be viewed as marginal.

74. If you need to place a hex just out of reach by an inch, then slip the Dyneema cord around until the bar-tacked section is pressed up against the nut.

75. If you have a mix of hexes and cams, then always use the hexes at belays and save the cams for when on lead, as a cam is always easier and faster to place.

76. If you get a wide crack you can try and stack large nuts, either end to end, or by slipping one hex partly inside the other, or even by wedging a rock (stone!) between the hex and the crack sidewall. Any stacked nut should only be used as a last resort.

77. Big hexes, being quite heavy, are ideal for holding down slings on spikes where you would prefer them to stay put. There is nothing worse than committing to the crux move, only to hear the helpful shout of your belayer, 'your sling's come off'.

78. Tricams are much-underused pieces of gear, and deserve to be taken out of the 'esoterica' cupboard. Lightweight, cheap and very robust (they work in dirty or frozen cracks), these nuts can be used as cams or as nuts. The smaller sizes (0.5 to 1.5) are highly recommended, especially on limestone. *(Figure 1)*

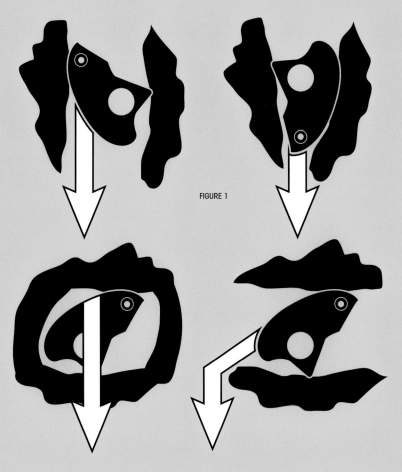

FIGURE 1

79. When placing a Tricam always give it a solid tug to seat the point into the rock, and extend it if possible.

80. In horizontal placements place the Tricam 'point down' so that the sling is wrapped over the top of the nut; this will give a much better placement.

81. To remove a stuck Tricam, hook your nut tool around the 'point' and give it a hard tug. To increase your tugging power clip a few extenders together and shock-load it out.

82. Like hexes, Tricams should be used on belays instead of your cams, as they are hard to place one-handed on lead.

83. Tricams can often be too floppy to place overhead into out-of-reach spots. Some climbers stiffen up the sling using electrical heat shrink (hold it high above a stove so that it shrinks without melting the tape!). You can also make it stiffer by adding a strip of plastic (make a strip from a heavy-duty milk bottle or drinks straw).

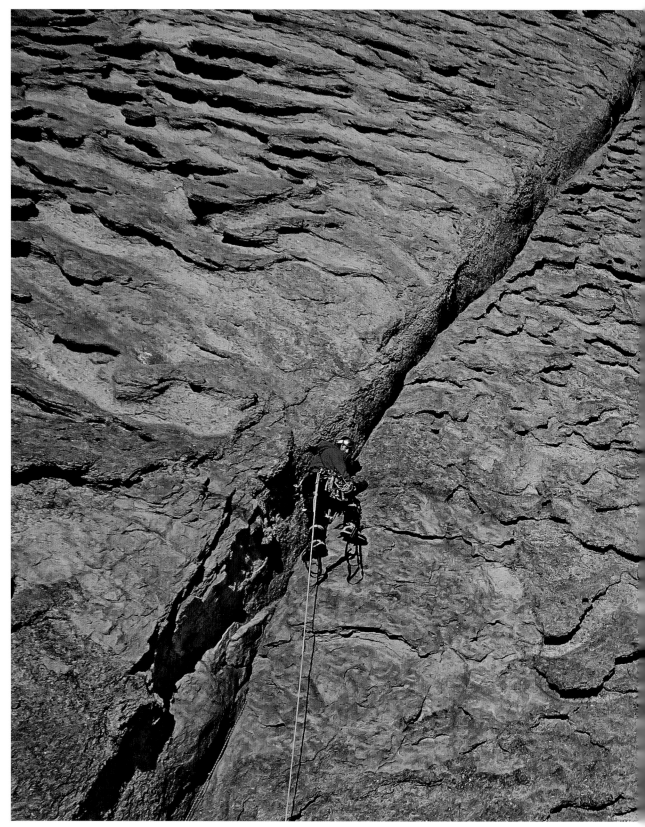

Kjersti Eide leading on Ulvetanna, Antarctica.

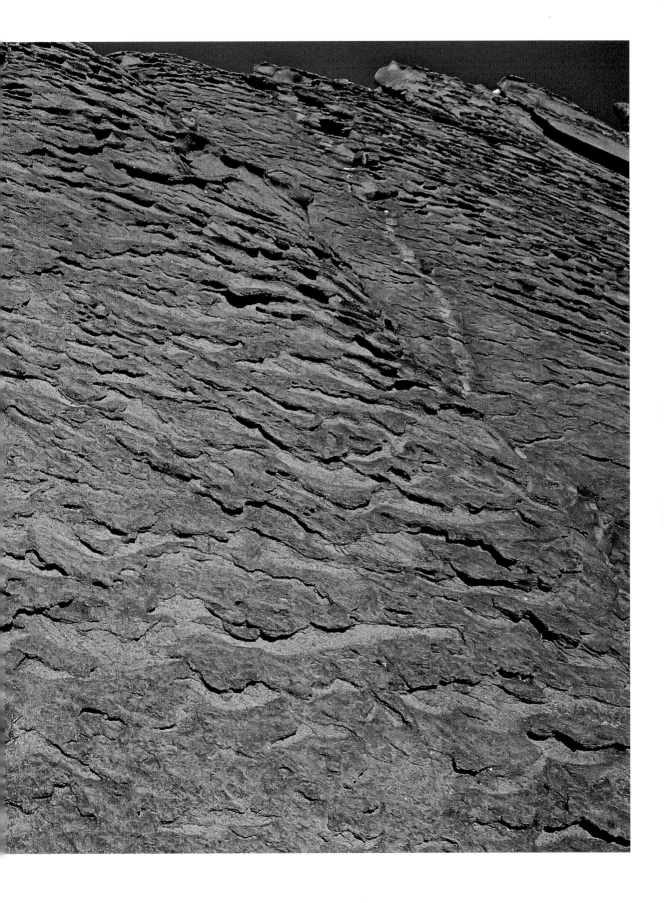

ACTIVE PROTECTION (84–95)

84. Treat your cams like a Marine treats his rifle; keep them clean and free of dirt, as you depend on them to stay alive. Grit, salt and dirt will reduce the locking action of the cam, and can lead to failure. Clean your cams with lukewarm water and a toothbrush, then dry them, and finally add some lubricant. I use WD-40, which some people say actually attracts dirt, but even if it does, it just means you'll clean them more, which can only be good.

85. If your cam's axles are damaged or the heads are deformed, then bin the cam, as most designs require all the cams to be fully functional in order to work.

86. Store all cams in a separate bag when travelling to the crag, rather than just throwing them into the bottom of your sack. This will stop the cams getting battered and twisted which can cause the cables to break.

87. The main reason a cam will stop working is due to the trigger cable breaking. If this happens mid-route there is very little you can do, apart from trying to hand-place it, but on multi-day climbs or trips you need to be able to repair the cam. Always carry a few metres of 1-millimetre kite Dyneema and 2-millimetre Dyneema, as well as some thin cable and swages. With this you should be able to make running repairs on your cams. You can crimp swage with a Leatherman tool or a rock and a nut tool (stick the nut tool on the swage and bash with the rock).

88. The more cams you place, the more of a feel you get for them; you soon realise that a cam can be rubbish one way, but great another. The main thing to remember is that the outside cam lobes should always be going on the widest area of rock (vital on shallow placements).

89. With a cam you're trying to achieve three points of contact, with the two wide cam lobes opposing the two narrow lobes. You actually only need three cam lobes in contact for a cam to work, so if the two outside lobes are good, and only one inside lobe is camming, then that's still a good placement.

90. Cams are faster to place and remove than nuts, making them the gear of choice if you're trying to climb fast.

91. Double-axle cams have many advantages, but their main one is that they have a much-reduced chance of becoming stuck. Why? I have no idea, but I just know that they always come out.

92. If a cam is stuck then focus on the cams themselves and ignore the trigger, using your nut tool to jerk the individual cam lobes loose. (Usually it will only be one or two that are stuck.) Work out which ones are moving, and then focus on those that aren't.

93. Sometimes you can force a cam all the way around, so the stem is in the inside of the crack, and just pull it out.

94. If the cam is totally stuck, then you can try hammering the cam sideways into a wider spot (a cam is not a cam when going sideways, it's just a lump of alloy). To do this place your nut tool over the axle and bash it with something heavy (large hex or rock) until it moves.

95. Remember that many cams become stuck, but few remain stuck for long, so just be stubborn – they always come out in the end.

SLINGS, QUICKDRAWS AND CORD (96–111)

96. Always carry a range of quickdraw sizes, as this reduces the chances of 'biners being loaded over edges. These should range from medium-length 'draws (15-centimetre to 20-centimetre) to long 'draws (25-centimetre to 30-centimetre). Unless you're sport climbing, 10-centimetre 'draws are pretty much a waste of time.

97. Always include a mix of sewn express slings (slings sewn together to make a strong, quite stiff sling) and open round slings (just sewn into a loop with a bar tack). This increases your flexibility, as express slings are stronger and keep their karabiners well orientated, but generally only allow one karabiner at each end, while open slings can accommodate multiple krabs and a long one can be clove-hitched. (Always carry at least one 30-centimetre open Dyneema sling.)

98. Organisation is key when it comes to slings, and if possible try to use a set colour for each size; such as grey for 240-centimetre, red for 120-centimetre and purple for 60-centimetre. If I had my way I'd make it an EU directive, like cam colours, as there's nothing worse than using someone else's rack and finding at the belay that the rat's nest of slings you thought to be a 240-centimetre is in fact several 60-centi- metre slings. By having set colours you should get the right sling first go, and it's vital when it comes to racking slings on your harness instead of over the shoulder.

99. Rubber retainers are recommended for the rope-clipping 'biners in extenders, as they stop the 'biner spinning around, potentially causing cross loading. Petzl Strings are best for this (those little black rubber things), but elastic bands or 'castration rings' also work very well until they perish.

100. I try and avoid ever having slings around my body, as they invariably tangle up, and can be a hazard in a fall. Instead, I make all 60-centimetre slings into quickdraws. To do this, clip a 'biner at each end, then simply pass one 'biner through the other and clip this back into the loop that's formed. This gives you a 20-centimetre extender that can be lengthened by unclipping one strand of sling and pulling. Avoid using rubber karabiner retainers on these quick-slings, as they can create a dangerous situation where you think the karabiner is attached to the sling when in fact it's only hanging from its retainer! *(Figure 2)*

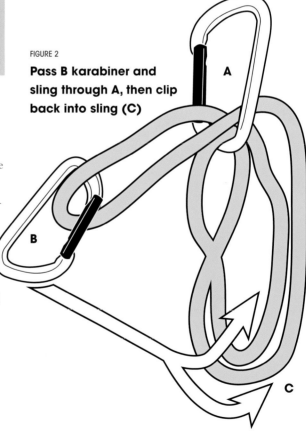

FIGURE 2

Pass B karabiner and sling through A, then clip back into sling (C)

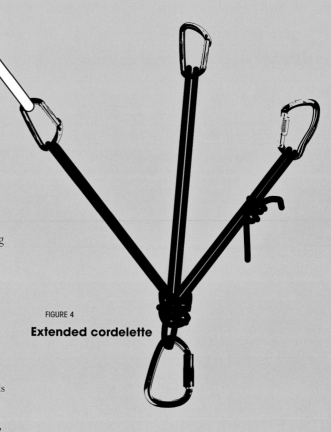

101. For long 120-centimetre slings I clip a karabiner into one end, pass the sling through the karabiner once, and put my finger through the three loops and twist it up and clip these loops into the karabiner (giving a sling one-third of the length when spiralled tight).

102. Cordelettes are good for complex belays, or when climbing in a team where the second(s) may not be climbing through (meaning you don't want to use your ropes to set up a belay). With a cordellette you can create a single 'powerpoint' from all the pieces in the belay for everyone to clip in to. To make a cordelette take six metres of 6- or 7-millimetre Perlon and form a loop using a double fisher-man's knot. To create a belay, clip the loop into each piece, then draw the strands down to a single point (where the force will be directed up to the pieces) and tie all the strands with an overhand knot. Clip a large screwgate into this to create the powerpoint. The climbers can clip into this point, keeping the ropes free. *(Figure 3)*

FIGURE 4
Extended cordelette

FIGURE 3
Standard cordelette

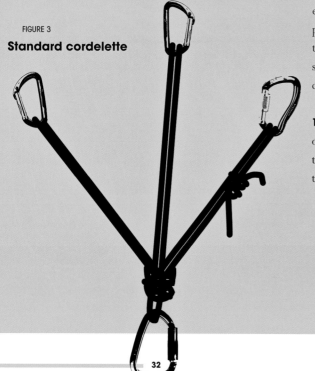

103. I've used cordelettes on belays so complex that I was equalising ten separate pieces to one point – with no one piece being solid, but as a whole it was OK. In these situations, your cordelette will not be long enough, and far pieces should be extended with a sling to reduce the distance the cord must travel. *(Figure 4)*

104. If you still don't have enough cord, or have run out of slings, then untie the double fisherman's knot, and simply tie a figure-of-eight into the ends and clip each one to the furthest pieces.

105. Instead of having a cordelette, simply set it up as tip 104, as a 'snake cord' – a 6-metre length of cord with two figure-of-eights pre-tied in each end. On trad belay setups just clip the two figure-of-eights into the furthest pieces. One bonus with this setup is there is no troublesome knot which invariably ends up in the wrong place when you are tying your main knot. *(Figure 5)*

106. Some climbers leave their cordelettes untied when racked, while others tie them with a double fisherman's knot. A good way to cover both bases is to tie the two ends together with a reef knot backed up with a double fisher-man's knot. This way it's a solid knot that is still easy to untie after being loaded.

107. If you want to reduce the clutter at the powerpoint karabiner, perhaps to clip off a rucksack or set up a haul system, then you can clip 'biners above the knot, through one strand of each 'arm' of the cordelette. This is called a 'shelf' and can be very useful.

108. A cordelette serves more than one purpose, and it can be used for creating a rescue spider (a sling with three arms for simultaneous abseils), as abseil tat, a super-cord-elette (you tie two cordelettes together to form a 12-metre sling) or simply as a massive sling to tie around big chockstones or over large spikes.

FIGURE 5
Snake cordelette

109. To rack cordelettes some people form them up into a super-neat little tight coil (make a small coil around your hand around 30-centimetres round, leaving about 40-centimetres free, then use this top wrap around the coil, passing the end through the end of the coil to tighten). Others just form a 50-centimetre coil, tie a figure-of-eight in the middle and clip both ends into a karabiner. I prefer the simplest method, which is to create a shoulder-width coil, then, leaving your fingers in each end of the coil, simply twist the whole lot a couple of times and clip both ends into a karabiner. This creates a tight bundle of cords that is quick to untie and won't leave strands hanging down behind your bag that invariably get snagged on your feet or rocks when you're descending. *(Figure 6)*

110. You can buy 60-centimetre, 120-centimetre and 240-centimetre slings, but I would avoid 240-centimetre and use a cordelette, and only carry one 120-centimetre sling, and four or five 60-centimetre slings formed up as quickdraws *(tip 100)*.

111. One very handy quickdraw to have is a long stiff one, basically a 30-centimetre quickdraw that is made stiff enough that it can be used to clip gear or bolts higher than you can reach. This can be achieved in many ways, from simply putting a length of wire next to the sling and wrapping it with tape, or using a strip of plastic (from a cheap plastic Tupperware-style box) heat shrunk to the sling. The clipping end needs to be taped in place so it won't flop, and the gate needs to have a system for keeping it open. On mine I super-glued soft Velcro to the spine, then wrapped a slim length of hard Velcro around this. When I want the gate kept open, I thread the thin Velcro through the wiregate and hold it open by wrapping it around the spine.

FIGURE 6

Shorten up

Twist

Clip both ends

Vanessa Sumner on Pywiack Dome, Tuolumne Meadows.

KARABINERS (112–123)

112. Use a mix of karabiners, both big and small, as this gives you more flexibility, but make up the bulk of your rack with small wiregates. Using primarily sub-30-gram wiregates will cut your overall rack weight by a large margin.

113. Mark all your karabiners with enamel paint (or spray paint) over the karabiner's spine where the strength is stamped. This area will retain the colour long after electrical tape has fallen off.

114. Carry at least one super-strong forged karabiner to use in situations when the krab is forced into a non-ideal loading scenario.

115. If you cannot afford to have your rope unclipped from your 'biner (say this is the only piece protecting you) then either use the small screwgate from your guide plate, or double up the wiregates. Old-style, bent-gate karabiners had a much higher chance of the rope unclipping, and even though wiregates tend to be fine 99 per cent of the time, why take the risk?

116. Karabiners in quickdraws should be easily identified as the rope-clipping end and the gear-clipping end, with one being 'soft' (only ever clipped to ropes and slings) and the other being 'hard' (only ever clipped to wires, pegs and bolts). I tend to have silver krabs for clipping into metal, and coloured krabs for clipping into ropes. Doing this will avoid the danger of a top karabiner with a bur on it (caused by falling on to bolts or wires) damaging your rope.

117. The top krab in a quickdraw should always face towards the direction of the pitch, meaning the bottom one will face away. The rope should then be clipped coming out of the karabiner – not into it. This will reduce by a huge degree the chances of the rope unclipping.

118. If a pitch is going straight up then switch direction with each clip, and if you're really worried then flip the rope 'biner upside down or add a screwgate.

119. If you're carrying spare 'biners, then clip them into bunches; two krabs side by side clipped into another two side by side. This way you can carry four or six krabs without taking up too much room.

120. Throw away any screwgate karabiners with a gate that can be over tightened, leading to jamming. A modern design should still have movement when tight (moving a millimetre backwards and forwards), while a poor one will be locked solid. What often happens with this old design is that when you have both people hanging from it on a belay, someone will notice it's 'not shut' and tighten it. What has happened is that the krab has opened up a little, giving some more play in the screwgate collar. Once the time comes to undo, when the second is alone and the krab unweighted, you will need the strength of Hercules to release it.

121. I'm a very big fan of twist auto-locking karabiners in anything but winter, as I know they are always locked, unlike a screwgate that can come undone at inopportune times. All such karabiners feel fiddly at first, but once you've had them for a while they're easily operated with one hand.

122. On long pitches DMM Revolvers can be a lifesaver, with their little built-in pulley wheel reducing drag on the rope. They also decrease the impact force on runners, and so are recommended on micro or marginal gear. (Plus having a krab that doubles as a pulley gives you an extra string to your bow.)

123. On a wet day, when you've nothing better to do, try setting up a karabiner brake using four karabiners. To do this, place two krabs together, gates opposed. Press a bight of your rope(s) through these krabs. Clip two krabs (back to back, gates together) into the bight(s), and back into the strand(s) before they enter the first two krabs. These are your 'brake-bar' karabiners. Now slip these krabs over the first two, so that the rope is running over the spines. Clip a screwgate krab through the first two krabs and clip this into your belay loop. This karabiner stops the whole lot falling apart. When you pull the ropes through at the end of the abseil, it's easy to drop the brake-bar krabs, so to avoid this clip a wire into them and back into your screwgate. *(Figure 7)*

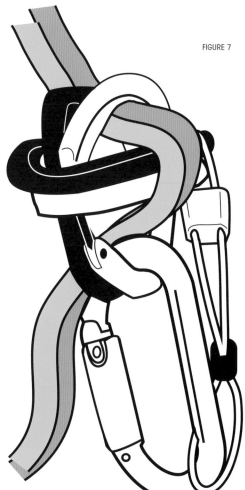

FIGURE 7 **Two opposed karabiners (gate against spine) set to keep primary karabiners in place**

Two karabiners back to back (ropes running over karabiner spines)

Wire used to secure primary brake karabiners to avoid loss

Neil Chelton battling his rope on the Eiger Nordwand.

BASICS (1–240)

KNOTS (124–137)

124. There are lots of knots out there, and learning many of them is part of learning to be a climber, with knowledge of things like a 'trucker's hitch' or 'Gordian knot' coming in handy now and again. In reality you really only need to know a few knots, and for me they would be in the following order: 1) Figure-of-eight. In my opinion the best way to tie in for all forms of climbing. Many feel that the bowline is superior, as it's easier to untie, but then having a knot that ties me to the rope that's a bit stubborn to undo seems like a bonus. 2) Clove hitch. Vital when it comes to adjusting belays. 3) Overhand knot. **The** knot for joining ropes for abseil anchors. And that's it! To be fair, being able to tie a few other knots is handy (see below), but really, if you just learn these then you will be fine. (I'm taking it as a given that you can tie your shoelaces.)

125. A double fisherman's knot is an important knot for joining thin cord together, such as the cord you find on old-style slung nuts and hexes. Always make sure you have a tail about ten times the cord's diameter. If tying Dyneema you'll need to use a triple fisherman's knot, as the cord is super slick and can slide apart under heavy loading.

126. Although I don't tie in with a bowline, being able to tie one on a bight comes in handy if you need to tie your rope directly in to a tree or boulder without using karabiners.

127. A Munter hitch is a good knot to know if you find you've dropped your belay device, and it can be used both for belaying and abseiling, although for descent you're better off using a karabiner brake, as the Munter will twist the rope. The Munter is great for fast belaying when on alpine-style terrain and you're belaying directly off an object, such as a spike: just throw a sling over a spike, clip in an HMS karabiner, tie a Munter hitch and away you go. To brake with a Munter you need to bring both strands together, not apart like a belay device. *(Figure 8)*

128. A variation of the Munter hitch is the super-Munter, which is the best knot there is for lowering heavy loads in a rescue situation. To tie a super-Munter, simply tie a Munter and then tie another one over the first. This knot actually kinks the rope less, as one knot puts in a kink and the second takes it out. With this you can gain a great deal of control. *(Figure 9)*

129. When using a Munter always make sure the braking rope (the one in your hand) is oriented towards the spine of the karabiner, not the gate, as having your braking rope running over the gate can cause it to unclip.

130. If you have to do a long, multi-rope lower then tie the ropes together with an overhand knot and lower via a Munter hitch using the largest HMS karabiner you have (a good reason to carry one oversized HMS). As the knot draws close to the Munter you will be able to force it around and through (make sure you push the tails through as well, and be prepared to force the two knots apart once the overhand knot has gone around the karabiner), saving you a ton of time and hassle – especially if you have someone who wants to get to the hospital stuck on the end. I used this technique to lower 100 kilograms of haul bags, six rope-lengths off the Troll Wall, and it is a real time-saver. *(Figure 10)*

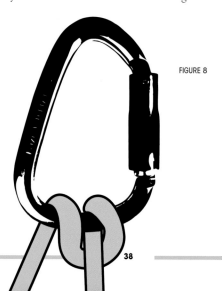

FIGURE 8

131. To get a clove hitch with the correct length, loosely tie the knot and, when the length is correct, just put your thumb on the first pass of the rope around the karabiner and pull the loose end tight to lock down the rope.

132. Whatever kind of belay device you use, practise tying it off in order to free your hands – before you have to do it for real.

133. If you have a knot that can't be untied then there are a few things you can try. If you hammer the knot with something heavy (rock or hammer) the knot will become deformed and it will loosen. Just make sure you don't hit it too hard.

134. The other method is to roll the knot backwards and forwards under your feet, again applying enough weight so the knot is deformed.

135. You can whack the rope against the floor.

136. Use your teeth.

137. For any knot that will be severely loaded, the best knot to use is an alpine butterfly. No matter how tight the knot, simply press the two 'wings' backwards and the knot will come undone (this is why the alpine butterfly is beloved by cavers and big-wall climbers).

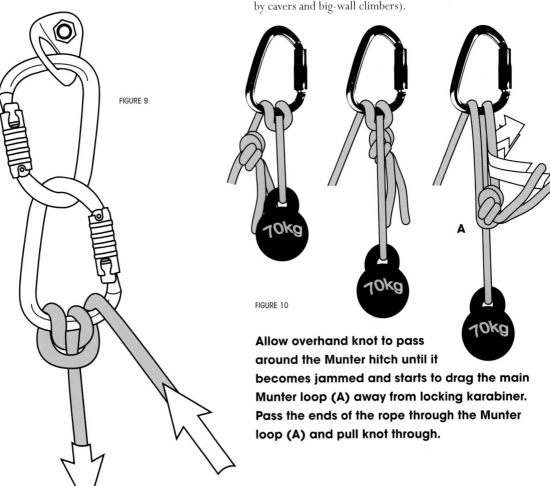

FIGURE 9

FIGURE 10

Allow overhand knot to pass around the Munter hitch until it becomes jammed and starts to drag the main Munter loop (A) away from locking karabiner. Pass the ends of the rope through the Munter loop (A) and pull knot through.

LEADING (138-142)

138. If you're on a pitch with spaced gear, or just one or two pieces, then don't trust your life to a single runner clipped in to a non-locking gate karabiner. Gear can fail due to such things as the rock breaking, some manufacturing defect (I know people who have had the heads of cams pop off!) or the rope can magically unclip itself. First of all, if one piece is all you can get, then treat it with all the care and attention that your life (or at least two unbroken legs) deserves. Make sure it's placed perfectly, extend it so that it stays that way, and clip the rope with a locking gate or two back-to-back krabs. If possible, place multiple pieces and create an intermediate belay.

139. Get over the fear of falling an extra inch or two. A 10-centimetre extender may reduce your fall by a whopping 10 centimetres compared to a 20-centimetre extender, but using a 20-centimetre extender instead decreases the chance of the gear being plucked out by the rope by 50 per cent. The longer the extender the more secure your gear will be, you'll have less drag, and the safer you'll be all round. Reaching for that 10-centimetre extender is just short-termism, and the second you're above it you'll wish you'd gone for something longer.

140. No matter how easy the climbing, always place gear. After all, if you're tied to a rope and carrying a rack, what's the harm in having a little insurance? Holds can break, feet can slip, or you may find a hard move with no pro, so having gear below that you placed when you really didn't need it could save your ass.

141. A good skill I learnt from climbers better than me was the ability to climb down as well as up. I noticed that climbers who did well would climb up placing gear, then down-climb and have a rest, then blast up and climb the crux. Often it's the placing of gear that tires you out, so doing this first and then focusing on the climbing is a great technique.

142. When you set off leading you need to know you have everything you need with you, and where you want it. Going half-cocked, with your rack just shoved on any old gear loop is both bad gear-wise, but also bad mentally. You need to feel as competent and able as possible. If you climb like a pro you'll feel like a pro – and you'll be a pro!

HARNESSES (143-187)

143. When you buy your harness, try it on with the clothes you'll most likely be wearing when climbing. Avoid jeans or anything with heavy-duty seams (these will rub you raw on multi-day routes).

144. When getting the correct fit it's vital that the rise – the bit that joins the legs to the belay loop – is the correct length to support you properly. If your body is too long and the rise is too short, the harness waist belt will be pulled down and be uncomfortable, and in a fall too much force will go through the belt. Too long and the belt will rise up, which can be dangerous if it interferes with your ribs. A good harness should fit the legs well, with the belt on the waist above the hips sitting straight and not under tension from the belay loop.

145. If you're buying a harness, ask the shop assistant for a bunch of quickdraws and clip them on and off to check its racking system.

146. Don't buy a harness from a shop that doesn't have somewhere for you to hang from while wearing the harness, such as a rope attached to a beam. When hanging, don't expect it to be super comfy, as hanging for more than a minute in any harness is grim (that's why we have belay seats). Instead just check that the harness is not digging in anywhere and that most of the weight is held by the leg loops, with the waist belt supporting your body, so you don't fall upside-down.

147. Try and avoid clipping a belay device or any large object into your rear rack or into a haul loop, as this places a dangerous object near your spine. Take a fall backwards or hit the deck and it will break your back.

148. I'd also avoid ever clipping a chalk bag to the back of my harness, as a chalk bag needs to be mobile so it can be slipped around the body when climbing chimneys or descending.

149. Using full-strength cord such as 5-millimetre Dyneema for your chalk bag means that you can tie into this as well as your harness, giving you an extra level of protection (just in case!). It can also come in handy if you want to rap off it, make a prusik loop, or clip into a rope if you get into trouble soloing and you aren't wearing a harness (remember that hanging from a piece of 5-millimetre cord will see you unconscious in a few minutes).

150. Use a combo of loose chalk and a chalk ball to get a good mix for climbing.

151. Always stow your chalk bag in a mini roll-top dry bag. This will stop the inside of your rucksack getting filled with chalk, as well as keeping the chalk off your spare clothes and kit.

152. If you want a quick system for indoor climbing, then replace your chalk bag belt with a loop of 5-millimetre bungee cord. This way you can just step in to the cord and pull it up like a pair of shorts, with no knots to tie.

153. The belay loop is among the strongest parts of a harness – so trust it!

154. Always carry a prusik loop on your harness for self-rescue. To save a karabiner, you can double it over and lark's-foot it to your rear haul loop or rear racking loop. As a minimum, carry one 1.5-metre-long, 5-millimetre-thick prusik. *(Figure 11)*

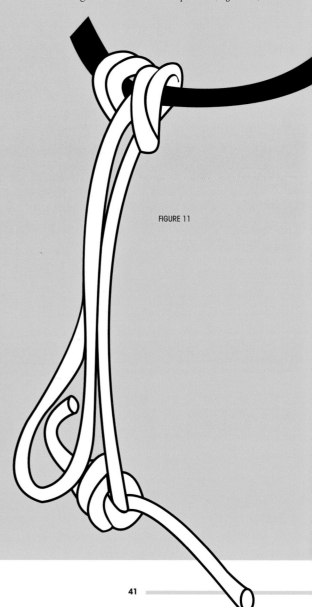

FIGURE 11

155. For multi-pitch climbing, add a second prusik of 2.5 metres as a foot loop, and also consider a lightweight ascender such as a Petzl Tibloc, Wild Country Ropeman or Kong Duck. These devices make rope climbing much easier and safer (they attach to the rope more securely), and can also be employed for many self-rescue techniques.

156. Keep all your prusik loops in good working order, as they are more likely to be employed as rap cord than prusik loops.

157. Many climbers carry a small knife on their harness; it's a good idea for when cutting rap tat or your partner's rope when they fall down a crevasse. Make sure it has a folding blade that is impossible to open by accident when attached to your harness. At the moment, the small orange Petzl climbing knife is the best, as it's a good size (some are too small) and it's sharp.

158. If you find you have to cut a rope and have no knife, then wrap a prusik loop twice around the rope and saw backwards and forwards. The friction will melt through the rope.

159. Daisy chains are useful on multi-pitch climbs, both for getting attached to belays, and even more so for rapping and cheating (aiding). If you climb as a three, they allow you to clip in to the powerpoint (the main point all the gear is equalised at) and untie from the rope if you need to swap ends.

160. The pockets of a daisy are also great for sorting gear. Simply take off the gear and clip each piece in to a pocket, allowing your partner to unclip it and clip it to their harness.

161. Never cross clip a pocket in a daisy chain (one 'biner through two adjoining loops) as the stitching between the two daisy pockets is only rated to around 200 kilograms, so if the stitches go, your karabiner will be unclipped.

162. To shorten a daisy, clip its prime 'biner (I always use a twist-lock) to the powerpoint, then get the correct length by attaching a second karabiner from your belay loop to the correct daisy loop. If you want to lengthen or shorten the loop, you just unclip this second 'biner. This way you won't have to open the gate of the prime 'biner to clip the correct loop (which would mean you're no longer connected).

163. When using a lanyard like a daisy, **never** climb above the powerpoint, as this could result in a high-energy fall that could break a karabiner, snap a sling, or at the least give your hips something to remember. Slings, be they nylon or Dyneema, do not absorb much energy, so try and view falling on them as you would falling on a length of steel cable.

164. Do not use adjustable slings (Petzl, Yates, Metolius) as your only connection point at a belay. These slings are low strength due to the buckle and can easily break under even moderate loads. If you use one, always stay tied in and have the tie-in point as your main connection to the belay.

165. If you use a daisy chain, avoid wrapping it around your body when you don't need it, as what will invariably happen is when clipping gear to your harness you'll cross clip the daisy as well. The best method is to clip two spaced pockets of the daisy into its screwgate and simply clip the bunch to the side gear loop.

166. If you use a 'guide plate' such as a Petzl Reverso, rack the device on an HMS karabiner and clip a second small screwgate krab to this as well. This means if you want to use the device in auto-lock mode, you have a mini screwgate at hand. (Avoid using non-locking krabs in this set up, as they can become unclipped from the rope, meaning your second will be totally unbelayed). *(Figures 12 & 13)*

167. On long multi-day climbs, always carry a spare, basic belay device. It will weigh very little, but if you lose a belay device it will be a real lifesaver, both for ascent and descent.

168. To avoid dropping my belay device, I have a piece of cord (a single strand of 3-millimetre cord tied with cinched fisherman's knots at each end) that runs from the release hole (the small hole) on my Petzl Reverso to the karabiner. Although this can add a slight level of tangle to belaying, it does mean that I haven't dropped a belay device for a long time.

169. Another way to reduce the chance of dropping a belay device is to feed the rope through the device while clipped to your belay loop, rather than removing it and threading the rope in.

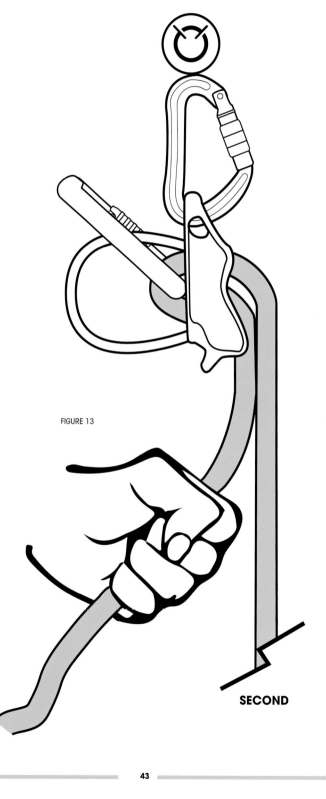

FIGURE 13

FIGURE 12

SECOND

170. A 'guide plate' is the only belay plate any multi-pitch trad climber should use, as it can be used for belaying, light hauling and rope climbing (used with a long prusik loop). Spend a few hours playing around with it at the crag, so that when you need to use it if for a reason other than belaying, you're up to speed.

171. Come up with a system for racking your gear on your harness and stick to it. Avoid the temptation to just clip it anywhere and go, as taking an extra minute will pay dividends once you're on the sharp end.

172. My personal approach to racking is (I'm right handed): wires front right; small and medium cams front left; big cams and long quickdraws back left; and small and medium quickdraws, belay device, spare screwgate, cordelette and nut tool rear right. The aim is to get some balance between the two sides, while allowing you to find the right piece quickly.

173. If you're carrying a big rack, then consider using a chest racking system like a Black Diamond Zodiac gear sling. This helps to prevent what would be a heavy harness falling around your knees when climbing long pitches, and it can also be swapped easily to the next leader.

174. Some people like using bandoliers, but I would always go for something like a double gear sling as mentioned above, as having all your rack on one sling can make you feel off balance, the gear can get tangled up, and, worse still, you can drop the lot in a fall! I once fell and got caught by the gear sling on a spike, which nearly ripped me in half.

175. One place where a racking sling/bandolier works is for the second, as it can be clipped off to the belay and the gear re-racked more easily than by having to remove it from the second's harness.

176. When seconding, try and re-rack the gear as best you can, quickdraws removed from cams and nuts, and all wires placed on one 'biner.

177. Never just let gear build up on your rope as you second. It's lazy and can lead to trouble as it could become jammed as you climb.

178. If you take out a nut with a quickdraw, always clip the nut end of the quickdraw to your harness. This way the nut and 'draw hang side by side, not full length, which again could result in it jamming as you climb.

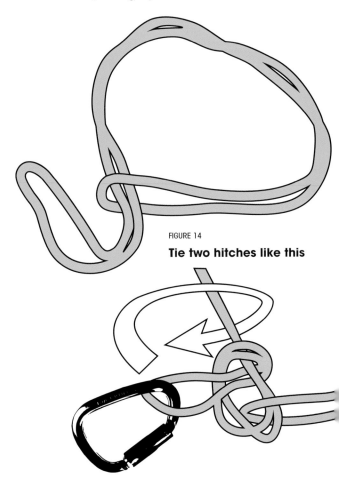

FIGURE 14

Tie two hitches like this

The author on the Russian route on the Eiger.

179. If you sleep a lot in your harness (on big walls and alpine rock), and there is no real chance of falling at night (you're on a big ledge), then I find that it's nicer to sleep in just the waist belt. If you want to remove the leg loops of modern harnesses, you'll need to separate the leg risers (often sewn together) and cut the retainer tab that holds the belay loop in place with the leg loops. Cutting this off will, of course, void your warranty and allow more travel along the leg loop front risers, but personally I find it is worth the modification.

180. An alternative to sleeping in a harness is to simply take it off, a luxury when you've been toiling in it all day. If there is still some risk – say you may sleepwalk off a ledge – then make a simple waist sling. To do this, take a 120-centimetre sling and pass it around your waist, pass the loop through the other end of the sling, pull it so that it's tight, then make a series of hitches clipping into the tail as your belay point. *(Figure 14)*

181. Avoid carrying too many screwgates on normal routes. All you should need are two big HMS krabs (one for belaying or attaching your guide plate to the belay, one to connect your ropes to the cordelette) and two small screwgates, one for your guide plate when in auto-lock mode, and the last as a spare. Beyond this, you're better off carrying extra super-light wiregates, and doubling them up (gates reversed) for maximum security. This gives you more flexibility.

182. If you're tackling a super-steep rock route, then consider taking along, or making, a nylon 'butt bag' – a fabric seat that will take some of the weight off of your harness. If you don't have one or can't make one, then at a pinch you can use a rucksack, clipping a sling from the waist belt to the haul loop. If nothing else, it's a great test of stitching!

183. If you want to carry your regular shoes with you for the descent, then just clip them to the back of your harness with a karabiner (first ensure the clip-in loop is strong and large enough). Better still, if the climb isn't too hard then just climb in sticky-rubber approach shoes.

184. A fifi hook is a very useful piece of kit for French free climbing or simply cheating. It also works well with a daisy chain to fine-adjust your position. It is best attached via a short length of cord around 20 to 30 centimetres long, tied directly to your belay loop. When not needed, you can tuck it away under the belt of the harness. *(Figure 15)*

FIGURE 15

185. On multi-pitch routes, you can use a second chalk bag to carry a small bottle of water, head torch, phone, Pertex windproof and an energy bar or two. Another option is to use a bum bag (or fanny pack if you're North American), as you can carry more water, a thermal top, hat, gloves, first aid kit etc. Using a bum bag or second chalk bag instead of a small rucksack means it can be pulled around to the front or side of the body for easy access while climbing, or moved out of the way when climbing a chimney.

186. If you use a bum bag, consider replacing the plastic Fastex buckle with a metal double-back buckle (you can buy these from outdoor fabric companies), as this will remove the chance of the buckle coming undone or breaking when climbing.

187. If you want a simple way of carrying a little extra insurance, stick an energy bar, a hat, and a head torch in the pockets of a shell jacket, and, holding the arms, spin the body of the jacket up to shorten it and just tie it around your waist.

BUILDING A RACK ON THE CHEAP (188–195)

188. Climbing gear is very robust, and so second-hand gear is generally fine; just stay away from soft goods such as ropes and slings.

189. eBay is a great place to find cheap kit, but be aware that people who steal kit from other climbers (from cars etc.) will try and offload it on eBay. Check the seller's details and history before buying anything. If it looks too good to be true, then it probably is.

190. If you're young and keen, then try your luck at getting free kit from older climbers, as older climbers tend to slowly amass a load of kit. Cheekily sticking a note on a climbing wall notice board saying, 'Young climber desperate for any old climbing kit', will probably find you nuts, cams and wires. Just don't expect them to be shiny and new!

191. The one item I would buy new, unless I trusted the person who was giving it away, is a rope. If someone wants to offload a rope for free it's probably because they no longer trust it, and if someone's selling it on eBay then you need to ask 'why?' If you search around you will probably find a shop that has a deal on.

192. Avoid cheap ropes if you're tackling big committing routes, and save them for outcrops and single-pitch and sport routes, as they will generally not handle well or be as well made as top-end ropes. You tend to find these ropes really cause you trouble when it comes to rappelling, as they will tangle and twist.

193. If you can't afford a new rope, then some specialist shops may have rope ends (the off-cuts from 200-metre drums of rope), or short ropes that will work in climbing walls and on single-pitch climbs. If you do buy a rope end or short rope, tie a knot in the end and tape it so it can't be removed, in order to avoid the deadly potential of the rope slipping through a belay device.

194. Although harnesses are soft gear they are very robust, and as long as one is not skimpy it will last a very long time. Just check that the webbing is in good shape and that it runs through the buckles well (modern self-locking buckle designs that do not need double-back buckles are much better, as repeated doubling back often leads to the webbing wearing out).

195. If you're climbing on outcrops and don't have a helmet you could make do with a cycling helmet; it will help in an impact fall (where your head strikes the rock). Just be aware that the parts of cycling helmets (buckles, cage, etc.) are not designed for the same stresses as climbing helmets.

INDOOR CLIMBING (196–208)

196. The place most climbers are likely to have an accident is indoors. The reason being that a climbing wall is a nice, safe, non-threatening environment. In reality, gravity works the same indoors and out, and this cosy indoor crag, with its top ropes and thick mats, tends to lower risk awareness, which can lead to accidents. First of all, at the crag your brain is usually more focused when leading, as the ground seems a lot harder (perhaps if walls had spikes or flaming pools of lava instead of mats, then they would be safer). There are also fewer distractions outdoors – no bloody awful techno music that tends to blare out in all climbing walls, people climbing left and right, conversations, people shouting or trying problems you can't do, or failing on ones you can, or the rush to grab a free rope and get leading before someone gets on your line. All this tends to create a complex environment where people forget to tie on, or forget to belay properly (how many people do you know who have forgotten to tie on outdoors?). The main point is to try to not be distracted when belaying or tying on. Have a set system for belaying and tying on, such as always tying on then tying a stopper knot (a good stopper knot should save your ass even if you half-finish your main knot). Use a belay device like a GriGri and learn how to use it correctly. Have fun but remember that gravity lives indoors as well as out.

197. People often feel embarrassed about warming up before they climb, but it really does allow you to climb harder and, more importantly, it reduces injuries. You just need to warm up slowly, doing light dynamic stretches (spin arms, rotate head side to side, twist waist, do some squats and swing your legs one at a time), then do a bunch of laps on an easy route, taking your time to feel your body wake up and stretch. Once you feel warmed up do some light stretches of your fingers (pull fingers back, or kneel on the floor with the weight on your palms, fingers rotated towards you). Taking a few minutes to work up to harder climbing will make climbing indoors more fun and easier on your body.

198. The classic mistake people make when starting out is scuffing their feet as they climb, wearing out the front toe section of their boots. Try and 'climb quietly' like a ninja, placing your feet as if the footholds are made of eggshell.

199. In order to improve your awareness of your feet, try avoiding using the toe of your boot, instead making use of the inside and outside edges, and the heel.

200. Many beginners actually ignore the toe of their boots as well, which can be a combination of unfamiliarity with climbing boots or how they are used, a lack of toe strength, or just a little too much focus on what their arms are doing. To get over this try climbing slabs without using your hands. You'll soon find that in most cases it's the feet and legs that power you up a route, and that your arms and hands just balance and hold you on.

201. Getting totally boxed in the arms with lactic acid (getting 'pumped') is part of climbing indoors, and part of getting stronger, but if you get so pumped you can't climb then you'll limit your training. Try to climb as quickly as possible to reduce the total time hanging on holds, especially small ones. At the same time you should work out how big a hold you need to rest and recover, which means dashing (in control) through a sequence of small holds, then stopping to recover on a bigger hold. Also, using your feet well and pulling your body in will reduce the load on your hands.

Photo: John Coefield

202. If you feel relaxed then you will climb better and get less pumped. Try and work out why you're feeling tense, and do something about it. The classic reason is a fear of falling, and you can combat that by climbing up and falling off as many times as it takes to get used to it. Once this fear is removed you'll climb a grade harder.

203. Try playing around with different hand positions when holding big holds.

204. Try to climb smoothly and in control; don't make super-long moves or daft high steps (save these for when you need them). Imagine you're in one of those old martial arts films, where the old master simply pushes the apprentice with one finger and they fall over – the lesson being one of balance. When you're moving you should be focusing on achieving balance in that movement. Like focusing on a single punch that puts you off balance, don't focus just on that next hold, but on your whole body.

205. The first clip is always the most dangerous, and it's here that people can break ankles, so make sure your belayer has plenty of rope paid out, and is ready to spot you if you fall before the clip. Try having the rope running over your shoulder, so when you get to the first clip, clip in the draw, then just grab the rope with two fingers on your shoulder and clip it in.

206. Some climbers try to reduce the chance of the first clip coming undone by making their first rope 'biner a screwgate. Although a little paranoid (a wiregate is fine), it is a good psychological trick, and screwing that collar up helps them relax.

207. If you begin to get pumped, try and get to a hold where you can take some strain off your arms and shake out. Shaking out with your elbows above your heart is more effective than doing it in the traditional way behind your back.

208. Try not to hesitate if you know what to do. You should fall because you fail to do the move, not because you fail to try the move.

BASICS (1-240)

ROCK BOOTS (209-219)

209. Unless you're climbing at the extreme end of things, having comfy shoes that are just 'tight' – rather than 'super tight' – will allow you to stay more relaxed when climbing, doubly so if climbing on multi-pitch routes. Aim to have your big toe slightly bent at the front, and a good close fit so the boot doesn't roll on your foot.

210. Don't confuse the pain of tight shoes with the pain of shoes that don't fit your feet. Slip new shoes on with the heel folded down first to check the toe profile is correct for your foot shape. After that you can think about length.

211. If you have funny-shaped feet then go for unlined boots that will quickly stretch to your foot shape.

212. You can accelerate the shaping of a boot by putting it in a plastic bag then dipping the front half into a pan of boiling water for 60 seconds (any longer and you may cause the glue to weaken). Then, with a plastic bag on your foot, slip the boot on and walk around and flex. This should help the boot shape to your foot.

213. If you have bits of your feet that just don't get on with your rock boots then visit a shop with a 'rubbing bar' (a bent piece of metal), and have them rub that area to stretch it out. You can do this at home with a blunt object and some arm power. Just make sure you don't use anything that will puncture the material.

214. If you're doing multi-pitch routes and want to be able to loosen your boots while belaying, then attach a thin strand of bungee cord through the clip loop at the back of the shoe and secure it around your ankle with a cord lock. This means that when you pull the heel off you won't lose your boots. Having two strands through a cord lock instead of a loop avoids the risk the loop accidentally clipping in to a runner while you're climbing – which would not be good! *(Figure 16)*

FIGURE 16

215. Resoling technology is getting better and better, but you need to get your boots resoled before they go through into the primary fabric or midsole. Once they start to go, it's worth buying a new pair, and getting your old ones resoled for use on big easy climbs where getting them trashed isn't too much of a heartache.

216. If you're climbing big multi-pitch rock routes in hot weather, then get very comfy shoes and fit them with socks, and even consider using an insole. As your feet swell you'll be able to remove your sock, but ideally they should be fitted so they are big enough to accommodate the sock as well, as this will help to reduce 'roll' in the boot caused by the inside of the shoe losing grip on a sweaty foot.

217. If you have a problem with smelly rock boots then sprinkle baby powder in them after each session.

218. If they're really bad and baby powder isn't working then sprinkle baking soda in them, stick them in a plastic bag and put them in the freezer overnight. In the morning empty out the baking powder and scrub them with a toothbrush.

219. If you really suffer from smelly feet, and in turn smelly boots and associated foot rot, then just use thin cotton socks and change them every time you go climbing.

ROCK CLOTHING (220–232)

220. If you're climbing on single-pitch routes then anything will do, from jeans and T-shirts to tracksuit bottoms and a tatty fleece. Personally, I think it's always good to have clothing that works well across a wide variety of conditions, and that will work both on a single-pitch route, or a big wall. Fit is vital; clothing should not be too tight or too baggy, and all materials must be up to the job.

221. Red and yellow are the best colours for photographs, with black and grey being about the worst, something worth thinking about if you want nice pictures.

222. Avoid materials that are slick and will reduce friction when jammed in chimneys or cracks. Fully breathable softshell fabrics made by companies such as Schoeller are perfect, as they are water and wind resistant and add a little warmth and weight, but still work well when it's super hot.

223. Make sure all fly zippers on climbing pants zip from the bottom up, so you can take a pee more easily when wearing your harness.

224. Trousers that can be rolled up either capri style (below the knee) or over the knee are perfect for multi-pitch climbing, as you can adjust their warmth this way as the day progresses.

225. A long-sleeved rock climbing top is ideal, as it will protect your arms when crack climbing, as well as from the sun and wind, but you can quickly roll the sleeves up to cool down. A good-quality base layer works best, plus go for a zip neck so you can cool off even more.

226. Make sure that any top you buy has a good length in the body, as short 'sporty' tops will quickly ride up out of a harness and this can lead to rubbing and chafing.

227. To avoid the seam of your trousers rubbing on your skin make sure they are long enough, so that the top of the waist sits just above your harness, and tuck your shirt in to your trousers before putting on your harness. I know it's super uncool, but it helps to prevent rubbing.

228. If you're going to carry a light fleece on colder days, then go with a design that has thumb loops, a hood, a long body and good arm lift. This one layer can work almost as well as a fleece, gloves and hat.

229. A light Pertex top is ideal, and better than using a thick softshell as it can be used over a base layer or a fleece.

230. Rock climbing tends to be a bit too difficult to do when it's wet, so most climbers tend not to carry waterproofs unless they're on a mountain route. Unless you're going to wear them while climbing, super-light (and even non-breathable) runners' waterproofs tend to work OK for emergency use.

231. Power Stretch bottoms are ideal for winter rock climbing, worn under your softshell pants, and they work from winter crags to major alpine faces.

232. If you want more warmth but without extra bulk on your arms, then a body warmer (vest in North America, or gilet if you're posh) works really well, and a lightweight synthetic one adds extra windproofing to your core without making your arms slick on cracks (although you may regret it if you have to belly flop).

Neil Chelton drop-kneeing on the Eiger Nordwand.

ROUTE FINDING (233-240)

233. Rather than carrying the guidebook with you, just photocopy the relevant page(s) and take that instead. If it's a big route then you can get it laminated and thread some cord through it. Another option is to take photos of the guidebook pages with a phone and/or camera which you can refer to on the route. (You'll have your camera with you on the lead, but maybe not your phone.)

234. Always have info on the adjoining routes, as this may help you work out where you are.

235. If the climb is in a mountain environment, then don't treat it like cragging; have the info and tools at hand to get on and off the route. This means a map (or section of map), tiny compass and full details of the descent.

236. Always make sure the team has a watch so you can judge your speed (make a note of when it will get dark). Watches are best attached to somewhere other than the wrist, as they'll get trashed and hinder hand jamming in cracks. I tend to put my watch on my gear sling or rucksack strap, setting it to beep on the hour to remind me to get my ass in gear.

237. When climbing a complex route, try not to let wishful thinking and an overly positive attitude lead you up blind alleys. Always route-find with a slight pinch of paranoia that you may be going the wrong way.

238. If you find you've gone the wrong way, either down-climb or get lowered back to the correct line. Don't be tempted to push on and then bring your second up, as this will probably compound your problems.

239. Knowing how to pendulum or tension traverse is a good skill on complex multi-pitch routes. If you're doing this in order to get back on route, you'll probably have to leave some gear behind. When using a single rope you will not be able to place any pro until you are above the pendulum point, due to drag, and it may be more sensible to make an intermediate belay, secure yourself, untie and pull the rope through the pendulum point. Just don't let go of the rope!

240. Tension traversing allows you to move sideways over ground that would be too hard to free-climb, and it's a good way to get back on to the correct line. The more you traverse horizontally the harder it becomes, so a slight downwards movement usually works best. The key though is good communication with your belayer. Try and keep communication simple, giving commands in feet or inches (or metric!), and shouting '**stop!**' when you want the rope to be held. The anchor you traverse off of also needs to be bomber, and it's worth making a mini belay (two pieces equalised), as failure would be pretty nasty.

Vanessa Sumner on Stately Pleasure Dome, Tuolumne Meadows.

Health and safety at Novo base, Antarctica.

002

SAFETY (241–327)

*"If it's windy, flake the ropes on two
slings attached to your harness."*

HELMETS (241–250)

241. In almost all situations, the first thing you should put on is your helmet, especially when you're approaching your route via tricky ground or where there could be rockfall. Having your head smashed in while a helmet is clipped to your pack would be very sad indeed.

242. Get into the habit of always wearing a helmet – it soon becomes as unnoticed as fastening a seat belt. A helmet not only protects you from falling rocks or gear dropped by your leader (or your leader!), it provides protection when you flip upside down after the rope gets behind your legs and many other 'head-first' falls.

243. If you're climbing a long route, which means starting in the dark and maybe finishing in the dark, then just leave your head torch on your helmet. Picking a small LED torch means it won't be noticed, but will be there and ready when the night comes on fast.

244. Make sure your head torch has new batteries, and if you carry spares then tape them together in the correct alignment so you can just plug them in all at once. This system also means batteries, dead and undead, stay together, and you're not left guessing which ones are which.

245. If you begin in the dark then get into the habit of checking each other's head torches are off once there's light. It's very easy to leave them on all day. (One good thing about LED torches is that they will probably last a few days even when switched on.)

246. To avoid dropping my head torch, which can happen when stuck head first in a crack or when pulling slings off my head, I run a loop of bungee cord through the vents in my helmet creating two elastic bands over its crown. When I put my head torch on, I pass the strap through the cord before securing it on the four clips. Now even if it pops off the clips, it will stay attached to my head.

247. If you're using your helmet for winter climbing then make sure you try it on wearing a balaclava, and also see how well your jacket hood fits over it.

248. For winter climbing you're generally better off with a hard-shell helmet, as ice hitting a soft helmet will damage it more quickly.

249. If you use a soft-foam helmet then never sit on it (well, never sit on any helmet), always put it in your rucksack last, and carry it with you on planes as hand luggage to avoid it getting broken.

250. When gearing up or stripping gear on a snow slope with any kind of angle, remember the guides' dumb client mantra of 'happy turtle' (helmet with the crown facing up) and 'sad turtle' (helmet with the crown facing the snow). If you follow this, you will avoid your helmet sliding away and being lost.

DESCENT (251–268)

251. On multi-pitch abseils, make one person the leader. This person fixes every belay and carries all the rack and the best head torch. By having one person do the whole descent setup, everyone gets into a rhythm and sticks to one system. Also, on difficult descents, the leader will get a feel for how the terrain will unfold, where anchors will be best built, etc. The leader should also have two mini ascenders (Tibloc, Ropeman etc.), if available, so they can climb back up the rope if needed.

252. Always keep hold of the rope ends rather than chucking them down with knots tied in the end. Attach both ends separately to your belay loop. This makes it impossible to rap off the end (knots can be forced off a rope in a high impact fall with the traditional system of just tying a knot to the end). This also means you only have at most 30 metres of rope looped below you (with a 60-metre rope), reducing the risk of damaging the ropes if you knock anything down. When you near the end, you may get some twisting. If this happens, just unclip the ropes from your belay loop and carry on down and they will untwist.

253. Never rappel below a loop of rope that's hung up – **ever**. The rope may not come free, leading to all sorts of problems, or, worse still, whatever is holding the rope may break away and land on your head. Instead, go down slowly and make sure your ropes behave.

254. When attaching the rope ends, tie a figure-of-eight knot for the 'pull' rope and a simple overhand knot for the other to remind you which rope you're supposed to pull.

255. Extend the rappel device from your harness with a secure quickdraw (replace karabiners with screwgates), or with a sling or a daisy chain. This gives you far more control over the device, as you can move your hand directly under it. If you use a 120-centimetre sling, tie a knot halfway and clip your device in the bottom loop and add a screwgate in the top loop (for clipping in and out of belays – similar to a daisy chain).

256. Always use a klemheist or autoblock (also known as machard tresse or French prusik) as your prusik loop and either clip it in your leg loop, or, better still, in your belay loop if using the extended system (*tip 255*).

257. Once the next anchor is built, the descent leader should give the rope a test pull to check the rope will run OK. If it doesn't move then they can do something about it.

258. Once the leader is sure the anchor is good, they should feed the 'pull' rope through the anchor, then clip both ends and do a 'gorilla call' – a low-pitched '**uggh**' noise (literally make a series of super-low-pitch gorilla calls). This tells the others they can come down, and it should always be answered with a 'gorilla call' to signify the message was received. This low-pitch noise travels further than a normal call.

259. If you are not certain about an anchor then bounce-test the piece(s) to check they hold. Also consider placing a backup that the last person down can bring with them (in such cases, make sure the last person is the lightest).

260. When it comes to pulling the rope, do it smoothly and under control, slowing as the end draws up towards the anchor and gravity takes over. If you pull really fast then the ends of the rope can whip up and become knotted. As you do this, feed the rope through the new anchor and take caution, as when the rope ends fly down your relief may be spoiled when they hit you.

261. On complex terrain, don't be greedy – do short 30-metre abseils with just one rope as this will reduce all sorts of problems (rope drag and a stuck knot for starters).

262. Tie ropes together with an overhand knot and no other – and if that's a problem then simply grow a pair. An overhand is the lowest-profile knot, and it will run over edges much better than any other knot. **Never tie a figure-of-eight knot**: joining two ropes with a figure-of-eight knot has killed or injured many climbers, as, unlike a simple overhand, it can easily roll and unravel.

263. If it's windy, flake the ropes on two slings attached to your harness.

264. If your ropes are different diameters, then it's worth noting that a skinny rope will pull through a belay much easier than a thick one – important on full-length raps – while a heavier rope will fall straighter if it's windy. If it's super windy, then lower the leader on both strands using your belay device or a Munter hitch. When rapping into steep and unknown terrain where the leader may need to jug back up – maybe a few metres to a potential anchor they have rapped past, or all the way back to the belay – tie off both ropes with a figure-of-eight (one on each strand, as this reduces twists compared to tying both together, and they are easier to deal with). This will allow the leader to jumar on either rope. Once they have an anchor, untie the knots so they can do a 'test pull'.

265. If you need more friction and control over your ropes, add a second karabiner to your belay device or simply wrap the live end of the rope around your leg.

266. If you have any worries that you may encounter a high level of friction when you rap, then leave a karabiner at the anchor with the rope threaded through it, as this will reduce the drag as the rope pulls through the anchor (a karabiner will offer a lower friction surface for the rope than if it were running over tape).

267. If the rope is very hard to pull, get your mini ascenders out and use these to increase your pulling power.

268. What do you do if one of your ropes gets damaged by a falling rock or a sharp edge and you need to rap off? For this, take your damaged rope and tie an overhand knot on a bight (**not a figure-of-eight**) at the end, making the loop nice and small. Now pass the good rope through the anchor and thread it through the overhand knot, creating a standard overhand rap knot, but with a bight and two tails (you would usually have just two tails). Clip a small screwgate from the bight in to the good rope (two opposed 'biners is safer). If you can, try and have the rope going through a small loop at the anchor, the idea being that the knot won't fit through. Now rap on the good rope (you will need to increase friction by adding more 'biners to your system if using a single skinny rope). Once you're all at the belay, pull on the damaged rope and drag the good rope down through the belay. (*Figure 17*)

FIGURE 17

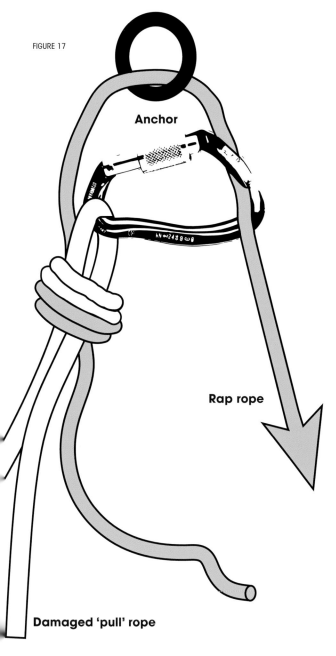

Anchor

Rap rope

Damaged 'pull' rope

DEALING WITH HEAT (269–289)

269. A super-hot environment can be one of the most dangerous places to operate, as you can lose your mind very quickly. Heatstroke and exhaustion (hyperthermia) can bring even the strongest climbers to their knees. If it's hot, then take it just as seriously as if it was -50°C.

270. If you're going from a mild climate to a hot one, you will need to acclimatise. This may take several days to achieve by slowly increasing your body's exposure to the sun and heat. To start with you may only be able to hang in the shade, but day after day try to give yourself an increasing dose of heat, then get back into the cool so adaptation can take place. If you intend to do something strenuous, make sure you do some strenuous exercise during this period, such as running up easier routes in the heat.

271. When it's hot, look at what the locals do and copy them: from how they dress to how they move. In a hot country, people don't move in the middle of the day – they get up early to get stuff done, or get out later at night when it's cool.

272. It's vital that you keep as much of your body covered as possible, especially your head. Wear long trousers and shirts, and attach a neck guard to the back of your helmet (or wear a sun cap with one built in). Stick sunglasses on as well, so only a small part of your body is exposed.

273. Any skin that is left exposed should have a high-factor sunscreen applied (including the back of the hands and ears), but sunscreen is no substitute for staying covered up.

274. When applying sunscreen, use the back of your hands and fingers to apply it so you don't get greasy fingers and palms. Also, sunscreen should be applied 30 minutes before exposure and should be re-applied every few hours.

275. Keep a close eye out for heat exhaustion in your team, which will appear as nausea, vomiting, delirium and a deep fatigue. If you suspect someone is suffering, then help them hydrate and cool off as well as you can. If you're on a big wall and can't go anywhere, and there is no shelter, then you should consider calling for a rescue or staying put (use a silver survival blanket as a tarp to hide behind), then retreat in the evening when it cools down. If everyone is losing control, then rapping off a complex climb in the midday sun will make things far worse.

276. Open-weave fabrics can provide low sun protection, meaning you can get burnt through a T-shirt or base layer. Check out the fabric's Ultraviolet Protection Factor (UPF) and go for clothing rated at least UPF 25.

277. Wear the lightest coloured clothes you can find, as thick white denim will be much cooler than thin blue nylon. On the other hand, dark colours get warmer but actually let less light through to the skin.

278. Keep an eye on the colour of your urine as an indication of how well you're hydrated. The lighter the colour, the more hydrated you are. Remember that pushing your body for long periods with insufficient water intake can quickly lead to kidney and urinary infections.

279. In hot weather, cotton wins out every time, as sweat will hang in the fibres and aid cooling, whereas with synthetic high-wick fabrics it will just go out into the atmosphere. Be aware that heavily saturated fabrics will allow more sunlight to pass through to the skin.

280. Try to pick routes that are in the shade for longer, or ones that are heavily featured (so there are places with shade).

281. Water rationing is vital, by which I don't mean drinking less than you need, but drinking only what is required to function. Keep a close eye on what you have, and make sure people take small sips often, rather than big gulps.

282. Add sports drink powder to water to replace essential salts and minerals. Plus the nice taste will make you want to drink more.

283. A classic alpine trick you can use anywhere is to carry a small plastic tube when you're climbing as you can use it to suck up meltwater that is running inside cracks.

284. If you're drinking plain water, then it's vital that you take up salts and minerals in your food each night to replace those lost.

285. If weight is not a problem, then food with a high water content or tins of food will help to increase your overall water intake, with tinned fruit being a great hot-weather staple on walls.

286. Many partners have pooh-poohed my liking of a can of Coke at night on a wall, but once you're up there, a mouthful of Coke really clears your mouth of all the gunk from hot weather climbing.

The author snoozing after a 'push' ascent of El Cap. **Photo:** Alwyn Johnson

287. Avoid alcohol and coffee, but do what the Bedouin do and hit the tea, either black or with milk, sugar or jam (jam in tea is popular with Russian climbers). The North Africans mix fresh mint with their tea as well, and drinking hot tea will increase your perspiration and create greater cooling (for this reason avoid hot drinks if you've stopped sweating due to dehydration).

288. On a big hot wall you can freeze your water beforehand. Water in the centre of a haul bag may stay frozen for several days, with water on the outside melting to drink.

289. If you find water that has been left behind, then take care; it could be very old and full of nasty bacteria. Take it with you, but use it only when all of your other water has been used up. If you have a stove, then boil it for at least one minute, or three minutes if you're above 2,000 metres.

LOOSE ROCK (290–301)

290. If you plan on doing adventurous climbs, get some experience in loose rock climbing, as suddenly finding yourself in the middle of a loose pitch where everything seems stacked like a house of cards is a steep and dangerous learning curve. Every country has its own brand of loose crags, so start there on easy routes and learn your trade.

291. Try to employ an ice climbing mentality for belays on loose pitches, placing them out of the fall line. Knocking your belayer out or breaking their arm is not conducive to a good day out.

292. Treat any gear placements with extreme suspicion on loose rock. If you're putting gear in to a crack, make sure both sides of it are substantial, as lightweight features such as flakes and blocks can easily be prised off in a fall – a cam can apply nearly four times the impact force to the rock.

293. When leading, you will often have to make a judgement call as to whether it is better to climb past potential protection placements in loose rock, or risk a fall that would bring rocks down on you or your belayer. If you really need to place gear, use passive gear (nuts) if possible to reduce the forces applied to the rock, and set up intermediate belays.

294. When a leader screams 'rock!' don't do what most novices do – look up to see if they're going to be hit. It's either going to hit you or it isn't, but being hit in the face is much worse than on the top of your head when you have a helmet on. When you hear 'rock!', press yourself against the rock and get as much of your body under your helmet as possible.

295. The 'three piece' rule for anchors probably needs to be doubled on loose pitches – and try to spread gear into as many separate sections of rock as possible. This means slinging spikes and blocks, nuts and cams, and fixed pegs all equalised. On such pitches, I've had up to ten pieces of gear tied together. Stand back and check the big picture before declaring yourself safe. Are those two vertical cracks and two horizontal cracks actually just one large shield of loose rock?

296. Never accept that a belay is crap. With modern gear, you can always find some new pieces, even if you have to first build your poor anchor, then use it as a runner as you lead up a short way into the next pitch, find a good gear placement, then climb back down and make that a part of the belay. Also don't be focused purely on what lies in front or above you, as often looking just around the corner can produce a nice surprise.

297. Always use double ropes on loose ground, and pay close attention to keeping both strands away from each other. If you pull off a block and it lands on one rope but the other is five feet away, you'll be glad they were apart.

298. Test all holds on loose ground by giving them a soft yank, applying bodyweight through your shoulder before committing your whole weight. The same goes for footholds, which should always be treated with care and respect.

299. Having an engineer's brain is a good idea when climbing a loose pitch, allowing you to scrutinise the holds or the layout of the pitch in order to judge the integrity of the move.

300. When approaching a crag, take the time to familiarise yourself with the ground. Most crags will feature a lot of blocks and boulders, but see if you can find small pieces of rock sitting on top of big rocks. This will often be a sign that there has been a recent rockfall, as small shards of rock tend to migrate off larger rocks through rain, snow and wind.

301. If a crag is known to be super loose, then make sure your approach is as safe as possible. If the approach is unreasonably bad, maybe you should consider climbing somewhere else!

The author on the Dru Couloir. **Photo:** Rich Cross

SAFETY (241–327)

RESCUE (302–317)

302. To avoid needing to be dug out of avalanches (dead or alive), attend an avalanche course and learn the skills needed to make good judgements in the mountains. And, more importantly, learn how to dig people out when those judgements turn out to be wrong. Many courses are subsidised and take only a day, so check with your national climbing body.

303. If you can't get to a course, educate yourself: buy and watch instructional DVDs, watch the many relevant videos available on YouTube, and read books.

304. If a number of you are interested in learning how to avoid getting caught in an avalanche, or in how to find those who have been caught, consider paying for a day with a qualified guide and get them to tailor it for your activity.

305. Take your survival seriously when going into serious environments in serious weather. Winter or alpine climbing is not cragging. Make sure you have the kit to move safely, and the kit to keep you alive if you can't make it back.

306. Always carry a shelter in the mountains. This should be something that the whole team can get into to share warmth and support (being able to laugh about your predicament is a vital component of survival). This shelter will take the form of a bothy bag (big nylon bag) and its performance can be improved with bivvy bags, belay jackets and food. Having one of these can be the difference between life and death.

307. Unless you're certain that all slopes are safe from avalanches, then each member of the team should carry a lightweight shovel (metal, not plastic) and an avalanche probe (and a beacon, if all members of the team own one), something that is done routinely by skiers operating in the same environments.

308. If you're climbing where you have to pay for rescue and medical care, then get insurance. If you avoid or delay asking for help because you may have to pay, then by the time you need it, it may be too late.

309. You should always carry out a self-rescue if you know you can do it safely and it will not expose anyone (you, your mates, other climbers) to undue risk. If in doubt, ring the mountain rescue, if one exists. What could take you several days may be done in minutes, and you can go from a full-on epic (mate with broken leg on the Eiger), to standing in the meadows within five minutes. Don't be hero – but also don't be a twat.

310. If you need rescue in Europe (including the UK) **dial 112**. You can do this from any phone, even a pay-as-you-go that is out of credit. Be aware that in many countries, including some European countries, there are no mountain rescue services.

311. Alternatively, get the number for the mountain rescue team that covers the area you're in. With this, you can ring them directly to communicate what your situation is and get advice. This can be a simple 'heads up', such as telling them that you have a slightly injured climber or that you're super dehydrated and not sure if you can go up or down. Around 99 per cent of the time, the rescue team will say 'hang on, we're coming for you', but when they're busy, it's good to let them know that you may need help.

312. Buy a cheap 'brick'-style, old-school mobile phone (pay as you go) and use this on the hill (inside two waterproof Ziploc bags). The battery lasts much longer than a smartphone, it's expendable, lighter and tougher (no glass.) Having a working phone with tons of battery in an emergency (if you have coverage), rather than something fancy with 1 per cent battery left, will save your ass when the mountain rescue team are on the other end of the line. You can also text the rescue services in the UK, but you need to register first. **Do it now**! Text 'register' to 112 and follow the instructions.

313. Helicopters aren't a magic bullet: they can't fly in bad weather, in mist or cloud, and they generally fly only in daytime. If you 'pull the pin' in the assumption that they will just be there in five minutes, well, you're wrong. They will prioritise your need for rescue, meaning if you ring because you fear being benighted, you may very well end up being benighted anyway. I've got several mates who died because the helicopter couldn't fly, and more who just got picked up in the nick of time. If you call rescue, don't assume anything, and have a backup plan.

314. Rescue helicopters in the Alps will often keep tabs on routes where they know climbers are operating and monitor how they are progressing. If one flies close, don't wave or make any movement that may be misunderstood as a signal. If you want to be rescued, then lift both hands above your head, arms outstretched, to form a '**Y**' for '**yes**'. If you don't want rescuing, then either don't do anything or just lift one arm up. *(Figure 18 – overleaf)*

315. If you do get rescued by a helicopter, put all your gear away, including ropes, and batten everything down. If at a belay, attach everyone to it by a sling, so they can just unclip and go. If you have goggles, stick them on. When the chopper comes, the crew will tell you what to do – and do exactly as they say. The main thing to remember is that you should only approach a helicopter when you are directed to do so, and always in view of the crew, and ideally in view of the pilot. On a mountain be very aware that if you descend to a helicopter on steep ground, the rotor blades may be able to strike you. Basically a helicopter is like a massive upside-down lawnmower, so treat it accordingly!

316. Very often, the rope man on a helicopter will be a guide – or there may be two guides (one to deal with each climber who needs rescuing). They may be 'long-lined' to you, meaning the helicopter will come and check your condition, then fly away, attach a long thick rope to the bottom, and then fly back with a rescuer(s) clipped to the end. Once they get to you, they will tell you what to do – follow their instructions to the letter. Usually, they will clip you in with a sling to the long line and unclip you from the belay, and, finally, they lift you off.

317. The most dangerous thing that can happen in a long line rescue, and which may jeopardise everyone involved, is for someone who is being rescued to be attached to the rock (for example, clipped in to the belay) when the chopper attempts to fly off. So make sure that you're clipped in with a single karabiner and that you unclip it when you are told to do so.

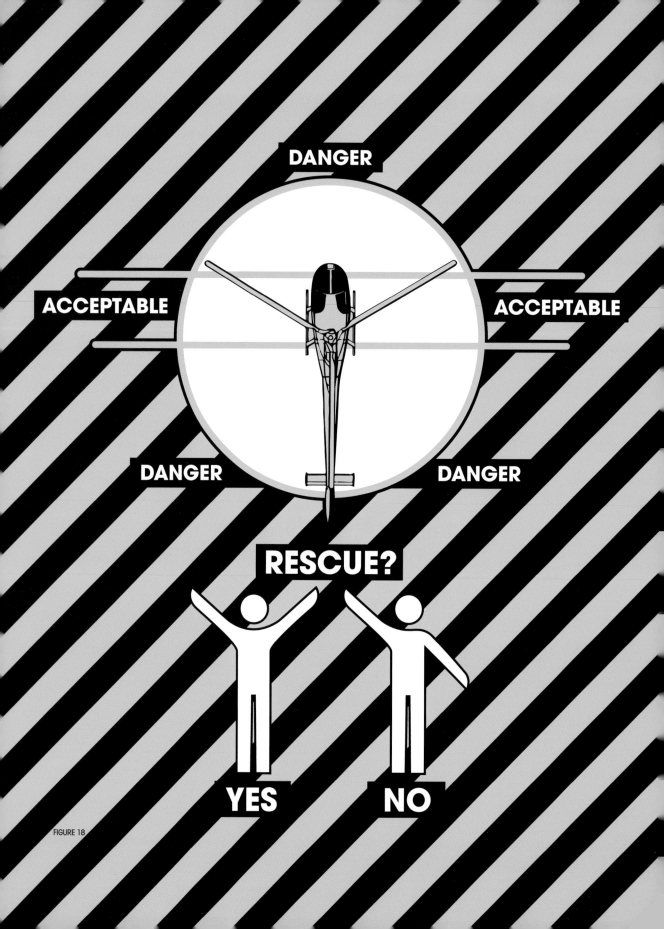

FIGURE 18

BENIGHTMENT (318–327)

318. The idea of an unplanned benightment on a big route is worse than it sounds, and it all comes down to how prepared you are: prepared for such an event, and prepared to suffer! I have had a few such experiences, and, luckily, I'm a paranoid type of guy, so I always had some gear to fall back on.

319. The first thing to think is 'can I just keep going?' Even if you see the sunset and sunrise as you climb, perhaps that might be better than stopping for the night. If you stop, but are not able to sleep, you will be much slower the following day. Having fresh batteries, and a little bit of food and water, may allow you to keep up the pace and make it to the top.

320. If you keep on going but are exhausted, it can get so bad that you may fall asleep involuntarily (I once stayed awake for over 40 hours: while climbing I would clip a runner, fall asleep, and then just wake up hanging from it!). If you get this tired, try to take a catnap for no longer than forty-five minutes. This will recharge your batteries and you will feel much better for another four hours. If you sleep over 45 minutes, your brain will fall into a deeper state of sleep and waking up again will be hard and you'll feel awful. The benchmark for sleep-deprived survival is a 15-minute catnap for every four hours you go into the red.

321. If you think you may get benighted, you will find it a little less traumatic if you add a few items to your kit. The first is a simple survival blanket or bag, either plastic or reflective foil. Make sure that what you have is light enough that you won't have to leave it behind, and that it's in good condition so it doesn't disintegrate when you get it out.

322. If everyone has a lightweight survival bag, then another object that will radically improve comfort is a bothy bag: a big nylon sack that you can sit or lie in. These bags are not breathable or even waterproof, but getting out of the wind and trapping team body heat in one place will make a big difference to your survivability.

323. If you need to secure the bothy bag to the wall to give you more space (i.e. so you don't have wet nylon flapping in your face), lark's-foot slings on the outside to nuts on the inside, trapping the nylon in-between.

324. Having something to sit on, or better still lay on, is good for an enforced bivvy. Just a square of foam or the padding from your bum bag or rucksack will make a difference. I often carry a piece of 3-millimetre tent underlay foam that is wide enough for my body and goes from my shoulders to my ass, cut into five sections and gaffer-taped together, designed to fit in my drinks bladder bag. I've used this several times and it works better than you'd think – well it does when you're so tired you'd sleep on a bed of nails.

325. Emergency under-insulation can be created with your gear, with the rope being by far the best. Just snake it around on the floor in the shape of your body and lie on it.

326. If it's going to be cold then spoon your partner. It may seem a bit strange at first, but very soon nature will take its course and you'll be thinking more about surviving than about any embarrassment caused by snuggling up with your buddy.

327. If you carry clothes for cold temperatures (enforced bivvies, storms or just motoring on into the night), go for gear that gives the maximum bang for their buck. I always carry a medium-weight fleece that features a good hood and fleece cuffs and is long enough to keep my ass warm. This design means you can get away without a hat. If I need more insulation (say I know I'll be sleeping on the route, but don't want to take a sleeping bag), then I'll throw in a light synthetic down jacket (with a hood) to wear over my fleece.

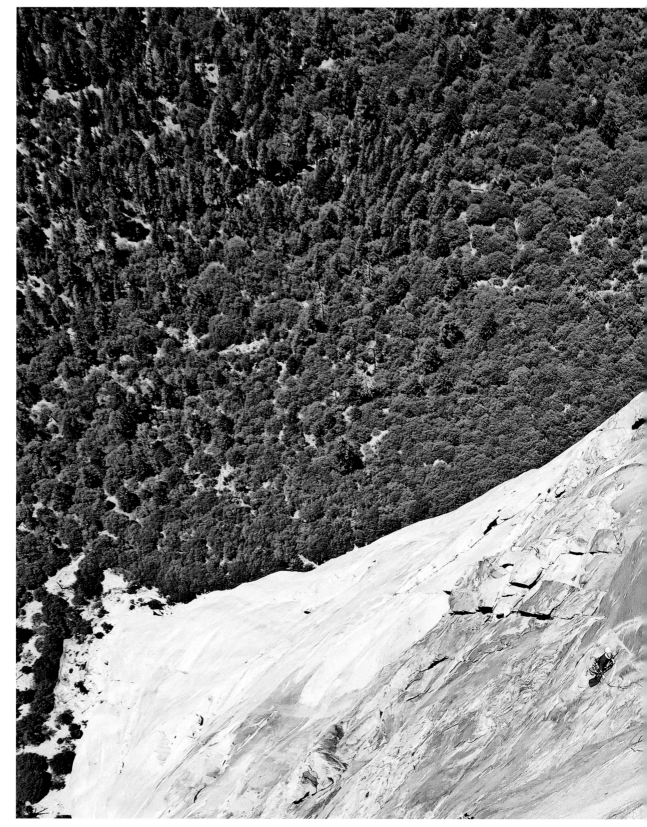

Charles Sherwood on *The Nose*, El Cap.

Portaledge bivvy on *The Nose*, El Cap.

003

BIG WALL (328-434)

"Never push a jumar tight up to any knot, as a jumar needs to move a few millimetres forwards for the cam to disengage from the rope."

PEGS (328–340)

328. The beak-style peg best typified by the Moses Tomahawk or Black Diamond Pecker, along with improvements in cams and nuts, has all but removed the need for any other style of peg. For most alpine, winter or big-wall routes, all that's needed beyond beaks are one or two baby angles, stubby Lost Arrows and maybe sawn-off angles. *(Figure 19)*

329. When placing any peg, first of all don't just view it as a blunt instrument; instead treat it like you would a nut. Can you get it to realise most of its strength simply by placing it in a certain spot? A good example would be a peg in a horizontal crack; just through the effect of leverage the peg should stay locked down tight, and hammering is only needed to lock the peg in.

330. Avoid over-hammering pegs as it can weaken or break them, and also damage the rock. For example, a solid pin in a crack, over-driven, can cause the sidewall of the crack to break off. Learn what it takes to make a good placement on a scrubby crag at ground level, using some slings to test it.

331. Always think about how the second will remove the peg, and never hammer them in to tight spots where the peg can't be hammered backwards and forwards, as this is the only way to remove most pegs.

332. File off any burrs from your pegs as these can damage ropes and slings.

333. When clipping fixed gear, always check that the eye of the peg is intact and not broken. If it is broken, you can lark's-foot a sling around the spine of the peg.

334. Fixed pegs can be bomber, but they can also be time bombs. How old are they? Are they corroded beneath the surface? The bottom line is don't trust them with your life. Back them up or just ignore them, as often they will have been placed before the invention of fancy cams and nuts and there may be a good crack not far away which you could lace with gear. This is doubly important at belays. (Many people seem to be happy to simply clip in to a single crap peg on a belay.)

335. If you're tackling big walls, learn how to use cam hooks, as these bent pieces of steel take the sting out of many pitches that would have once required many peg placements, saving time and gear. The Nipple pitch on *Zodiac* is a prime example; a pitch that once required several Lost Arrows in a row, hammered upwards into a roof crack. Now you just leapfrog two cam hooks along and do in a few minutes what once would have taken an hour. *(Figure 20)*

336. Beaks can be placed in horizontal cracks just like knifeblades (I no longer carry knifeblades) by placing the beak tip sideways, then tying it off with a sling through the head of the beak (to reduce leverage).

337. When placing a beak, always aim to get a good 'hook' before you get a 'constriction' between the metal and the rock. Very often, a solid beak can be wiggled out using just your fingers because it's actually hooking the rock so well.

338. Tie a loop of cord through the eye (or the head) of hooks so they are easier to rack, and use oval karabiners, as these have more room to hold the peg.

339. Spray-paint your pegs so you know which are yours and which are fixed. If you're doing a hard aid line, where you're carrying dozens of beaks, spray them different colours (small, medium and large).

340. On a lot of trade routes, you may need sawn-off angle pegs, and it's worth carrying a good size range. Invariably, these pegs can be placed by hand, saving the rock from being further damaged.

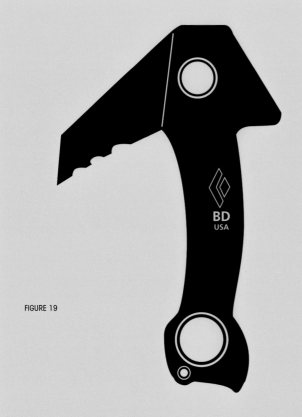

FIGURE 19

FIGURE 20

JUMARING (341–354)

341. Just like learning to climb slabs, cracks and steep faces, practise all forms of jumaring, including the FROG system (chest harness, Croll and handled jumar), Texas system (two handled jumars), Sport system (one jumar and a Croll), rope walking system (like the FROG system but with a foot ascender) and emergency systems (prusik loops and mini ascenders). Practise all on steep and slabby ground, so you can see the pros and cons of each, and cherry-pick the style that fits the pitch.

342. An important skill to master is the ability to take a handled jumar on and off the rope using one hand, with your thumb working the trigger. Using two hands is slow, which is a problem if you have to do it a few thousand times on a wall.

343. When climbing a rope that is unweighted (or there is not enough weight below you), as you step up on your top jumar the rope will be lifted up by your bottom one as you move it. Most novices will use their other hand to hold it down as they move their jumar up, which is inefficient, and the ideal is never having to take your hands off your jumars. To avoid this problem, as you push the bottom jumar up, slightly pull back the cam (**not** the safety trigger), so the rope just slides through without resistance.

344. Practise jumaring both up and down, with down-jumaring requiring good thumb/cam skills. This is a great technique to employ in a scenario where a rope is under tension and can't be threaded through a descender.

345. The length of your daisy chain to your top jumar is critical in the two-jumar Texas/Yosemite system. When hanging fully on the top jumar, you should be able to operate the jumar, meaning your arm will be slightly bent even when fully weighted. You can mark this distance with a marker or a small loop of 2-millimetre cord tied in to the pocket (tape will come off).

346. It may sound obvious, but many people don't realise that there is a left and a right jumar. The left jumar is the one that when in your left hand you can see the cam clearly, and vice versa. This also puts the cam so you can thumb the trigger.

347. The number one rule of jumaring is you must have two points of connection at all times. If you remove a jumar, then you have to be tied in (so one knot, one jumar). I've seen pro climbers' jumars pop off the rope many times.

348. If you're belaying with a GriGri, once the rope is fixed, just leave it and use it as a 'running knot,' with the next backup being your knot at the end where you're tied in. To start, you'll need to pull rope through as you climb the rope, but soon the rope will self-feed.

349. Traverses and lower-outs are the number one killer moves on walls for beginners, leaving the second stuck at the last piece of pro, a jumar either side, unable to unclip the rope. In this situation, just pass the gear with your top jumar, pull the rope tight through your GriGri so all your weight is on it, take off the middle jumar and lower out with your GriGri. As you pay rope through the GriGri, you'll transfer on to the top jumar and lower off the piece. Once the rope is slack, clip the lower jumar back on and swing back to take out the gear.

350. What do you do if you don't have a GriGri? Well, it takes some practice, but pass the gear with the top jumar, pull the rope tight with your hand below the second one, and thumb the cam back and allow the rope to slip through, which will allow you to lower it. This is actually faster than the GriGri method, but it takes more practice.

351. If you use a handled ascender for your foot and a GriGri for your body, you can quickly swap from jumaring to abseiling, making it popular for route setting and inspection, but also for when you've dropped your other jumar.

352. The FROG system of a chest harness and a Croll is good for free-hanging ropes, but when setting up your Croll you can just use a length of thick bungee cord – either a loop running from the back of your harness, or over your shoulder. Whatever system you use, the ideal setup will leave you stooped over a little bit when standing.

353. Never push a jumar tight up to any knot, as a jumar needs to move a few millimetres forwards for the cam to disengage from the rope.

354. Avoid the habit of clipping a backup karabiner through the head of your jumars as this just wastes time and is unnecessary for straight up jumaring and cleaning. Plus, you should be backed up anyway, either with knots or with a GriGri. The only exception is when passing gear where the rope is going horizontally, as the backup karabiner will stop the ascender twisting off the rope.

'Kiwi' Steve Bate soloing *Zodiac*, El Cap.

HAULING AND HAUL BAGS (355–375)

355. When using a Petzl Pro Traxion pulley, always clip a karabiner into the bottom so there is no way the pulley can open by accident.

356. Instead of using a plastic bottle top to protect your hauling knot, use a medium-sized fuel funnel. Remember to drill or melt a hole in it and attach a small prusik loop, so it doesn't get lost when you untie the rope.

357. Use an alpine butterfly knot to attach your haul line to your bags, so it can be untied no matter how loaded and tight it becomes.

358. If you clip your haul bag in with a karabiner, always use two karabiners with one on each strap, as the two straps can easily flip a single 'biner to get a three-way load (you may need to extend one 'biner with a second plain gate if using offset-length straps).

359. Swivels are really only necessary for routes that involve slabby hauling. *(Figure 21)*

360. When racking your wall hauler, either on your harness or when tagging it up, feed the haul line through the pulley first, and clip a small screwgate in to the end (with a fisherman's knot). This way, when you want to clip the pulley to the belay, you can first unclip the rope 'biner, pull it through the pulley, and clip it off to the belay. Now unclip the pulley and clip it to the belay. This way, you can't drop your haul lines.

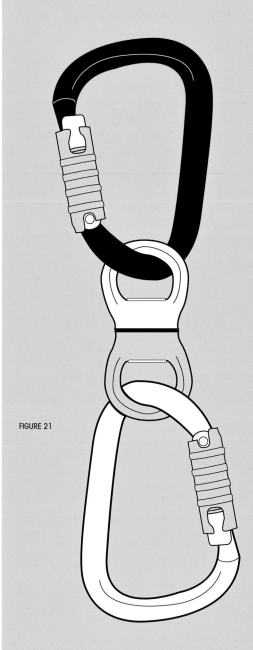

FIGURE 21

361. If you know you have to haul past a knot, tie the ropes together with a reef knot, backed up by a fisherman's knot, but make the tail of the bottom rope a metre long. When the knot is a few inches from the pulley, attach a jumar below the knot and lower the weight down on to it. Take the long tail and untie the fisherman's knot, tie an overhand knot into it and clip it to the belay, then untie the reef knot, pull the end of the old rope through the pulley, open the pulley and insert the new rope, and carry on hauling.

362. Line your haul bags with cardboard or thin plastic so that sharp objects don't press through the material and cause damage.

363. Try not to make the classic newbie mistake of packing your bag to descend, before remembering you haven't taken the carry straps out of the bottom!

364. Most people like to use static ropes for hauling, but I often use a dynamic rope, meaning I have a spare lead line if my lead rope gets damaged. The downside is that dynamic ropes are not as tough as static ropes, but, when hauling, once you have 100 kilograms hanging on the end their dynamic properties are minimal.

365. A thick haul line can be quite a drag when leading, and once you're over 30 metres up, it's impossible to get gear sent up unless you have a third rope, or a lower-out line. To avoid this, a tag line can be used, which is usually a half rope or dedicated tag line (5-millimetre or 7-millimetre cord). With this system, you can get all your belay kit (cordelettes, pulley and krabs) sent up as well, reducing the load on your harness.

366. Don't be lazy with your haul line. Always stow it either in a rope bag or loop it through the straps of the [haul] bag itself.

367. When it comes to hauling and the rope starts going up, be proactive and check beforehand that the rope will come straight from the bag and up to the next belay, and that it won't get caught behind crap on your belay. If you've attached it with two locking krabs, even if it is tangled you should be able to unclip, sort, and re-clip for hauling.

368. Remember that all actions have a reaction; meaning that when you untie that docking cord, or unclip that wall hauler, you should know the bag is going to do what you think it will do. Get it wrong, and the bag will drop 60 metres on to your belay, a force great enough to break your belay!

369. Hauling is much more than simply betting your weight against the bag; it is literally weightlifting, where you're often moving an object much heavier than you. Remember that wall hauling is not offering any mechanical advantage and is simply 1:1. If you can't move the bag by weight alone, you'll need to either use more muscle or more brainpower, but, no matter how heavy, your bags will move.

370. If you're forced to haul a super-heavy load, say you're a four-person team, or a three-person team hauling a lot of supplies (such as water), then keep the load below 200 kilograms. If it's greater than that, then split the load between two haul lines, and set up two different haul points. Splitting the load also works if you're light and soloing, or just a lightweight full stop!

371. Never clip your haul bag in to the belay with slings or a daisy chain, but rather tether it with a double strand of either 7-millimetre or 8-millimetre cord. To do this, take a 6-metre-long cord, 7- or 8-millimetres thick, pull the cord through the longest strap on the bag (or just pick one) until it's halfway through, and tie it off with a figure-of-eight knot. When the bag gets to the belay, simply take the two strands and tie a double Munter hitch, pull it tight and then tie it off. To tie off, simply wrap both tails in the opposite direction around the tight strand several times, then tie off with an overhand knot. Don't tie a quick release knot, as the result of it coming undone by accident could be terminal. This is normally referred to as 'docking'. *(Figures 22 & 23)*

372. As soon as the haul bags are docked and the haul line is removed from the pulley, clip the haul line off to the belay as a backup.

373. Check that your route doesn't traverse, and, if it does, then take a lower-out line. Thirty metres of 6- or 7-millimetre cord or an old half climbing rope works well, lowering via a Munter hitch.

374. If you find yourself on a pitch with a lower out but without a lower-out line, as soon as the haul line is fixed, clip the line off short (with an alpine butterfly), untie the end and use what you have to lower-out.

375. The necessity for a lower out is to avoid breaking your water bottles, plus having several hundred kilos of kit swinging on the end of a rope isn't good if you have any sharp edges.

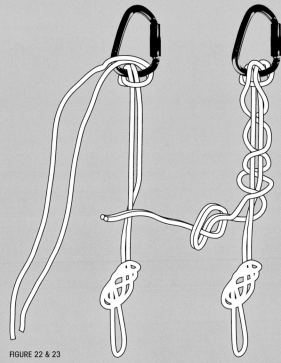

FIGURE 22 & 23

Haul bag docking cord

7-millimetre or 8-millimetre cord. Tie off with one or two overhand knots – **not** a quick release knot!

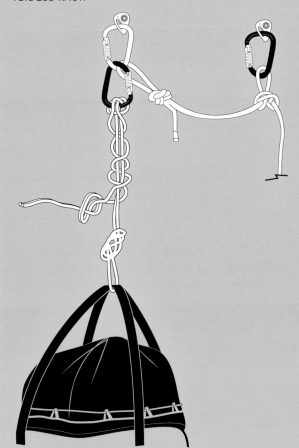

SPEED CLIMBING (376–398)

376. If you want to get fast, you don't have to actually climb fast – just climb. What you need to avoid is stopping (belays, food and drink stops, having a smoke, looking at the sun going down). If you reduce stopping time to the absolute minimum, then you will be fast – period.

377. Carry a watch on your harness and try to record how long it takes you to do things on average, such as: climbing a pitch, building a belay, and getting your mate on belay; how long it takes you to strip a belay; how long it takes for your mate to second; how long it takes to get the next leader off the belay and leading.

378. In speed climbing, the leader is the tip of the spear, and it's the team's job to keep that spear moving forward at all costs. If the leader is waiting for you to strip the belay, and second the pitch (clean) before they can lead, then give it everything you can. All actions must be focused on keeping the leader leading.

379. When seconding, pull out all the stops – as well as the gear – and don't be afraid to pull on gear, or even the rope, if that's what it takes to get up there and get the leader leading.

380. The first aid pitch I climbed on El Cap was graded A1, and it took me most of a morning to do, bounce-testing bomber wires as I slowly crept up a crack in total fear. Many years later I led ten pitches in around the same time when I climbed *Zodiac* in 18 hours (17 pitches). The difference? Well, I had the same basic understanding of the mechanics of how gear worked, and I had climbed several hundred more aid pitches, but really it was a change in my approach. I was speed climbing. I was a speed climber, and any doubt or hesitation or unfounded fear had no place in such a climber's mind. The same was true when I soloed the North Face of the Droites in six hours – I just had to free my mind of all the heavyweight shit that would hold me back. It's easier than you might think.

381. Learn to move together on easy ground, or get confident soloing together (if you have a rope and gear, then you may as well use it), as this will cut down your overall time.

382. Why speed climb? Well, apart from the thrill of moving through sketchy terrain as fast and as safely as you can, speed climbing is the fundamental principle of alpine climbing, and it will make you way safer once you've mastered it by reducing the time you're exposed in the mountains.

383. Practise moving together with the rope running through a Petzl Tibloc mini ascender as a literal 'running belay' to catch the second if they fall. If the leader falls, the Tibloc will not engage, and the fall will be the same as a normal leader fall.

384. Just because you're speed climbing doesn't mean you should forget to put gear in. The chances of falling will increase if you overdo it – trying a route that's too hard to be climbed quickly, or an easy route that you're trying to muscle up too fast. Stick the pro in and climb as if you're soloing (carefully!), as taking a massive lob will put a huge dent in your speed.

385. Learn how to 'short fix' if you really want to increase your speed, a system that all but removes the time lost when you're waiting for your second to climb up and put you on belay. The basics are you get to the belay, pull all the slack up, clip this tight from the second to the belay (leave some slack if they have to lower out on traverses), and with the spare rope you have, you begin rope soloing the next pitch (using a GriGri or just trusting you won't fall). Your mate now jugs up as fast as they can and puts you on belay as soon as they arrive. The spare rack is then sent up on a tag line or haul line.

386. When speed climbing, pay close attention to your nutrition and hydration, as you will be drawing a great deal of energy from your body, plus, in a push-ascent, you may be doing four or five days' worth of climbing in a single day. Carry enough water to see you through the day and night, plus the way down, and carry plenty of food that's easy to eat on the fly. My favourite is taking along sandwiches for every four hours, and adding energy gels and bars in-between.

387. The art of climbing a big route in a single push is to know how to spread the team's energy over the whole route. This generally means going steady to begin with, then speeding things up as you get into the groove, leaving time to finish the route in the dark – or in the light if you're fast.

388. Don't just think of an early start as meaning 5 a.m., as an early start can actually be as late as 7 p.m. – only the day before. If you're fit and psyched, then starting in the evening and climbing through the night will put you halfway up a route in the morning, and ideally at the top long before it gets dark. Often, when you start in the dark and it gets dark again, you really hit a bit of a wall.

389. Sleep is important on a push, and a three-person team is ideal, as you only have to lead a third of the route, and when one person is belaying, the other can have a kip, or a brew and generally a rest.

390. Try and avoid placing gear that is slow to place and remove, meaning nuts. Instead, carry more cams and make full use of them.

391. Trying to climb *The Nose* in a day? Doing it on sight is pretty rare for mortals, so climb it first over three days, going fast, but not so fast that you get shut down in a day and have to come down. Treat this as a recon for your one-day ascent.

Now have a week off and work out a strategy. Break the route down into two or three very long pitches and, by short-roping, moving together and with what you know about the route, blast it in a day, starting in the evening (when the wall is quiet and cool) and aim to be up on the upper wall by dawn. Simple!

392. A single rope is the only way to go for speed climbing, but don't go for something too skinny, as it's going to get hammered.

393. If you're a very fast leader, then consider a 70-metre rope when short-fixing, as you don't want to run out of rope before the second has started to belay you.

394. An alternative big-wall speed system is a three-person team, where the third climber jugs the haul line with a second lead rope, then begins leading the next pitch as the last person cleans.

395. An alternative is to go with the short-fixing method, and the leader pulls the lead and haul line tight, then the second climber jugs the haul line and takes over leading on the ends of the ropes the leader pulled up, while the third climber cleans. The good thing about this system is that only one lead rope is needed.

396. If you're going to be climbing fast at night, make sure you have plenty of light power, with the leader using the brightest light you have.

397. Always carry a spare head torch and batteries.

398. Don't embark on a big wall in balls-out speed style unless you know how to get down a big wall with your balls between your legs. Always have mirror plans for both success and failure, and have the tools to carry out that retreat (cheater stick etc.).

Aleks Gamme on the Troll Wall, Norway.

HAND BOLTING (399–413)

399. Always carry a blow tube so you can clear out the rock dust caused by drilling, and avoid getting any moisture in the hole until you're done.

400. Keep all your bolting kit in a bolt bag or chalk bag. Attach a screwgate to it and tether the drill holder with a leash so it can't be dropped.

401. Don't forget to carry the correct-sized wrench for the bolts you have, as a Leatherman tool or simply using your fingers tends to not work that well.

402. Tape a wrist loop to your wrench so it can't be dropped.

403. If you're using Petzl self-drive 8-millimetre bolts, carry a micro screwdriver in your bolt bag. This is used to clear out the core of the bolt if the rock debris becomes too compacted. If this isn't cleared, then the bolt will be much harder to drill, and the wedge may not work effectively. *(Figure 24)*

404. Always carry spare wedges for self-drive bolts, as they are easily lost.

405. On any big wall where bolts may have been placed, carry a number of 8-millimetre self-drive hangers, and know what the holes look like – they are easy to miss.

406. When drilling a bolt, go for one to three taps per second. Don't hit the drill holder too hard, as you'll damage the bit. What you're doing is slowly chipping the rock away, then turning.

407. Rock hardness is the biggest factor in drilling a bolt, and you can tell a lot about how hard it's going to be in the first few hits. See what works best to chip away the rock – try two hits then turn, or one then turn.

408. When drilling a bolt, make sure the rock is sound and not simply a flake or a loose pillar.

409. Practise drilling bolts before you attempt a route that may require them. Once you learn the technique, you can place them quite quickly, but until then it can seem like an impossible task.

410. If you're using 8-millimetre button head bolts (or wilderness bolts), you need to use 9-millimetre drill bits unless you're drilling in soft rock.

411. If you're establishing a new wilderness route, take the time to do it right by placing two 10-millimetre stainless steel bolts at belays and 8-millimetre button heads on lead. If you do use 8-millimetre self-drive bolts, leave the hangers on.

412. Use good quality drill bits, ideally Hilti SDS.

413. If you want a lightweight system for drilling emergency bolts, buy a 22-centimetre-long, 9-millimetre Hilti TE-CX bit and use the bit as both the drill and the handle by inserting some plastic tubing or hose pipe on to the bit to form a handle, as well as some cord to form a wrist loop. Use this in combination with Fixe 8-millimetre button head bolts and either stainless hangers or Moses lightweight keyhole hangers. This bit can also be used for placing rivets or drilling holes for bat hooks.

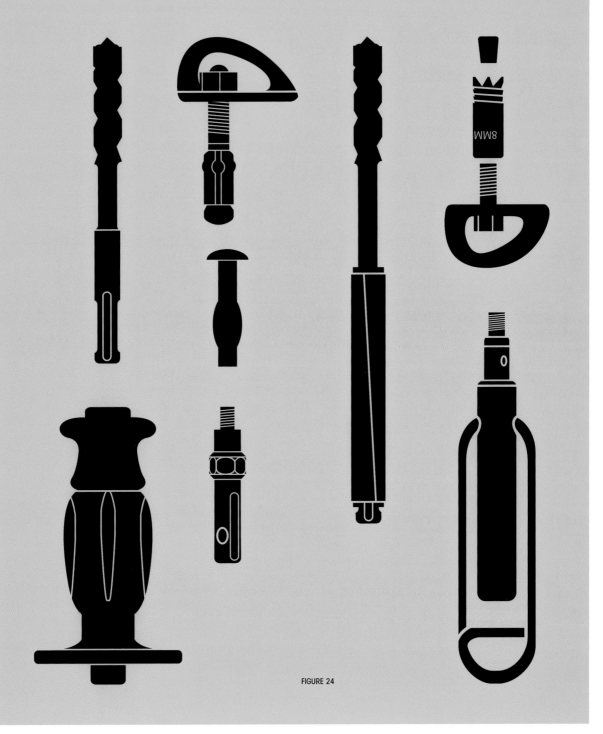

FIGURE 24

BIG WALL (328–434)

HOOKS (414–424)

414. If you're tackling a big wall, then the most important hook to have is a pointed Black Diamond grappling hook. This is an off-the-shelf hook that has the last inch gradually taped down to a dull point (don't make it sharp as it will just jab you in the leg). Having a point means it can go in to tighter spots and latch into divots in the rock caused by multiple people hooking the same spot.

415. Always use 5-millimetre Dyneema to sling your hooks, as it is far superior to webbing, being stronger, more robust and less likely to untie. Make the loop long enough that it doesn't cause the hook to move while you're hanging from it, but not so long that you lose too much height.

416. Beyond pointed grappling hooks, carry two Moses pointed hooks and two flat Moses hooks, as these will work better on super-small edges (matchstick size), with the flat hook spreading the load over a greater area (good on softer rock).

417. Some people also make a second style of modified grappling hook, sawing off the tip to create a flat hook for flat, round edges. To do this, you need to saw off the end of the hook just beyond where it begins to drop from its apex, and then file to a dull point.

418. When filing hooks, always use a hand file, and don't go mad and get the steel too hot.

419. Large hooks are good on some hard routes, but they are increasingly rare (the Fish hook can still be found, but Pika and Vermin no longer exist). An alternative is to just use size-3 beaks such as the Tomahawk, as these can be hooked over flakes and even taped into place. *(Figure 25)*

420. When hooking, don't look at the hook directly, as it will smash you in the face if it rips. Also, always wear a helmet, as your head will soon be running in blood once the hook has popped a few times and bashed you on your noggin.

421. Hooks can be tested like all other gear, just don't be too dynamic: apply body weight, think about it, apply a bit more (using a daisy chain or aider), then get on it.

422. Avoid racking your hooks in sets, so if you drop one krab, you won't lose all your hooks of that size. Instead, clip them into mixed sets, and always have a spare set on any major big wall.

423. A Black Diamond Talon is a good backup hook, as it features a pointed hook, a flat hook, and something between the two.

424. On a hard big wall, when there seems to be nothing, check that you're not missing any bat hook holes – tiny holes drilled to take a pointed hook like the Moses. These holes are poor style, but still crop up (these days when you drill a hole, it's usually filled in with a rivet, as bat hook holes wear out with a lot of traffic).

FIGURE 25

FIFI HOOKS AND CONNECTORS (425–434)

425. A fifi hook attached to your harness makes it easier to quickly clip in and out of gear, and for most big-wall climbing it's far superior to using a krab clipped to your belay loop.

426. When attaching the fifi hook, don't make the connection too short, as it will make it hard to clip it in to the gear. People do this because they feel like they really want to be super tight to the piece, when in fact most of the time, you're fine just having it extended by 25 centimetres. To easily do this, buy a 30-centimetre, 8-millimetre Dyneema sling and lark's-foot it through the fifi, then lark's-foot the fifi on to your belay loop.

427. If you need to shorten your fifi hook further, simply pass the fifi through the karabiner on the piece, then hook it back on to your belay loop, thus halving the distance.

428. On hard aid climbing, where you may have to do a lot of top-stepping, you might want to swap out your fifi for a karabiner, as you may need to be pulling it upwards (your waist is above the gear). You can easily do this by lark's-footing a 30-centimetre sling into your belay loop. It's worth locking the krab in place with a Petzl String or elastic band (or a slip knot) so that you know where the 'biner is.

429. When using karabiners for connectors, go with keyhole-style krabs so they don't snag on webbing or gear.

430. When not using your fifi, you can just tuck it in to your waistband. Some people sew a little Velcro tab on to their harness in order to keep it from snagging on gear as they climb.

431. If you use adjustable daisy chains then you all but remove the need for fifi hooks, as you can cinch the sling down to the same sort of distance.

432. The little hole in the head of a fifi hook is designed for a 'pull cord', used to more easily yank the hook off the gear. Either tie a single strand with a knot in the end (use bright cord), or a loop, which can be used to clip the fifi off to the side when not needed.

433. A fifi can be used for many more things than pure aid climbing, and one of the most useful for big wall stuff is the ability to leave your haul bag hanging from a fifi, before hauling it up later. This is a good trick if you're fixing ropes, as you can leave the bag on the end of the fixed rope, jug up it, then haul the bags (this means you're not forced to jumar a loaded rope). This of course means your haul bag is hanging from a tiny, $5 alloy hook so it could be viewed as high risk.

434. A Kong adjustable fifi is a popular fifi design for hard aid climbing, as you can adjust the length of the cord to fit the placement, making it easier to fine-tune the length.

Belay on the Russian route, Eiger.

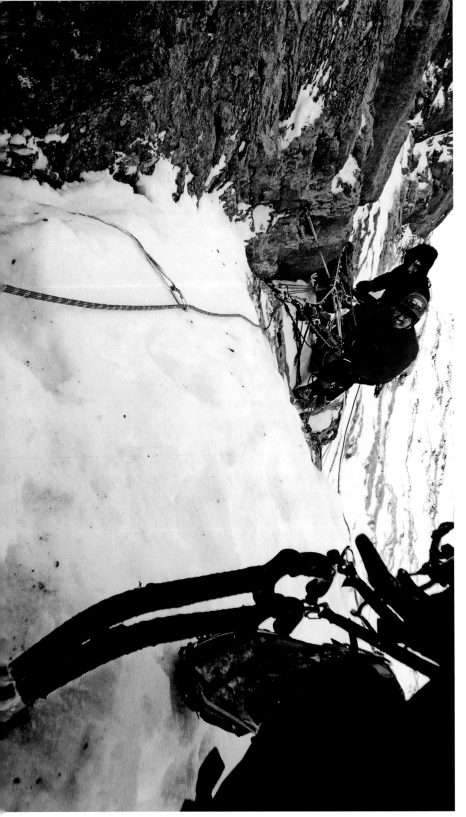

Neil Chelton at the sharp end on the Eiger.

004

ICE (435–481)

"Don't forget to visualise rests, spots where you can take some weight off your upper body, and ideally get some gear in at the same time. Imagine these as being like islands that you're swimming between."

Rich Cross approaching Cerro Torre in winter.

ICE (435–481)

BASICS (435–447)

435. Keep your picks sharp, and always have a file when away. (I use a tiny, flat precision file snapped in half, so it's only 2 inches long.) On some big, hard routes you may need to file the pick mid-route.

436. Ice climbing is primarily all about your footwork, and how much you trust your crampons – even though it will feel like it's all about your arms. It's worth top-roping an off-vertical route just using your hands and crampons to build up your confidence in your feet, and to see what they can do.

437. Try to only place your picks in spots that are concave (scoops, dimples, folds) as the ice is less likely to shatter there and will be at its strongest.

438. Look for lighter patches of ice, which contain more air, as you will get a good stick there.

439. Go leashless: it's easier, less pumpy, more fun and safer. (You place more gear, you pump out less, and you're less likely to fall off because you're able to move so much more fluidly.)

440. If you've not climbed any ice for a while, do a few minutes of bouldering at the bottom to remind your brain how a pick works and how to move on your feet.

441. Always use a lanyard such as a Black Diamond Spinner Leash with your axes, as this achieves the obvious in that you won't drop an axe, but, more importantly, you will be more relaxed.

442. Use lanyards that are full strength and will take a fall, as these can save your life if you're hit by falling ice while leading, or by heavy spindrift or an avalanche.

443. Replace the crappy karabiners at the ends of your lanyards with small, full-strength wiregates. You can use screwgates, but on wet ice routes you may find that water runs down your tools and freezes in the gates.

444. If you unclip your lanyards from your tools, then attach your tools to something else solid or rack them, as they are very easily knocked out of the ice by the rope.

445. When rapping or moving with my axes clipped to my harness, I generally attach them with a locker as they have a tendency to unclip themselves from karabiners.

446. Place one tool, then your feet, and practise just swapping hands and changing your hand position. You'll be surprised how long you can hang there.

447. If you want to push your grade, I would strongly advise that you go somewhere where you can top-rope as much ice as possible (like Rjukan in Norway), as pushing your grade on lead on ice is probably one of the riskiest things you can do. I would say you need to have twenty top-ropes under your belt before you try leading that grade (I'm talking about grade 5 and up), but then I'm obviously over cautious.

ICE (435–481)

PROTECTION (448–455)

448. If you're ice climbing abroad, then dump the rock gear, and, unless it says otherwise, just take ice gear – and lots of it. You'll need four screws for belays (two each), so on easy ice I'd carry an additional five, but on hard ice I'd carry an additional ten.

449. Only carry one super-long screw (22-centimetre) and make the rest up of stubby (10-centimetre), short (13-centimetre) and medium (17-centimetre), with the main types being medium and short.

450. Place your long screws at the start of the pitch when you have the most gas in your guns, and when the impact force from a fall will be the highest (less rope out), and use the short and stubby screws higher when you need a faster screw. (Short and stubby screws are still more than strong enough on good ice.)

451. Those plastic 'pan pipe' things that people carry screws in may look like a gimmick, but they work really well and I highly recommend them. Make a belt out of a Petzl adjustable lanyard or make your own full-strength belt (metal buckle and heavy-duty polyester webbing), and, once threaded in place, tape them on. This way you can't lose either a screw or a tube, or the whole deal if a buckle breaks.

452. When using pan pipes, thread a long sling through all the screws when on the approach or when they are packed, so that the screws won't fall out (and down to the bottom of the canyon) on the way to the start, or when unpacking.

453. Don't store your screws in pan pipes unless you know they are dry, and always protect the tips of your screws with good quality end caps (yellow Grivel ones are heavy duty).

454. Before you climb, spray WD-40 into your screws, so that the ice core slips out more easily when taking them out, and spray them again at the end of the day to avoid corrosion.

455. Mark your hangers with tape or paint so you know which ones are yours, and if they're not colour-coded, consider spraying the different sizes so you can ID them when they're in their tubes.

LEADING (456–481)

456. Before leading, take a moment to look at the line and work out where you will place gear, and climb the route mentally first.

457. If your aim is poor, then you can touch the spot where you want to place your axe first with the tip of your pick – then draw it back and place it properly. This allows your brain to memorise the movement before you commit to it.

458. If you begin to lose strength in your grip, you may find that your tool begins to lose its stability when you place it. To reduce this, place your thumb on the back of the shaft.

459. Don't forget to visualise rests, spots where you can take some weight off your upper body, and ideally get some gear in at the same time. Imagine these as being like islands that you're swimming between.

460. When leading, try and keep a positive attitude and verbalise this. When you get a solid stick, say 'train stopper', and keep your belayer up to speed. Avoid any negative language or thoughts. Often, if you climb with a novice who's a bit gripped, you climb better because you have to be positive on their behalf, while in a more balanced team you can just be relaxed. Look at the best climbers when they're climbing – they tend to have a very positive attitude.

461. You must not climb above your belayer – this is a golden rule of ice climbing – as falling ice can knock them out or break bones. 90 per cent of the time there is not a need to do this, and simply making a short, rising traverse off the belay will put them out of harm's way.

462. If you are in a situation where being hit is unavoidable, then at least try and place the belay at a point where you may milk a bit of protection from the terrain; say under a small bulge or tight in a corner.

463. You can also reduce your risk of being hit by clipping a pack above you on the belay and hiding under it.

464. When setting up belays, always keep your screws one axe length apart, as screws closer than this risk fracturing the ice. The standard safe working distance is 50 centimetres apart (most axes are 50 centimetres long).

465. Avoid ever placing your picks level with each other; instead offset them. And always try and keep them an axe length apart on fragile or super-cold ice, as you can easily cause a fracture between the picks that will see you take a lob.

466. Ice is formed by gravity, and so once it gets steep enough to climb on (and not just walk on) your feet should be 'parallel with the planet'.

467. Learn the modern 'triangle' method of climbing ice, where the pick is kept close to the body line and the feet are wider than the shoulders. This technique is super stable, fast and avoids barn dooring. The old 'X' method involved placing both axes side by side (bad!), running the feet up (putting maximum strain on the arms), locking off (again hard on the arms), then moving your axes up. Again, practise both methods on a top rope, but, like with getting a 'solid roll' for kayaking rivers, get yourself a solid triangle method.

468. Remember to 'swing like you screw, kick like you poo' – when you swing your tools, you need your groin pushed in to the ice, and when kicking you need your feet up and your ass out. This will reduce fatigue on your arms and keep your heels low.

469. When climbing try and maintain 'good form' – moving smoothly and in control. Be aware of this and use it as a signal that you're climbing well. The moment you become aware that you're losing form or getting sketchy, take a moment to consider your options. Can you rest? Can you belay and let your partner climb? Perhaps you need to clip in to your tool and place a screw and have a breather? Redlining on ice is a good way to get hurt, so try and climb as if your life depends on it.

470. When moving on ice, your arms will be in just two positions: either straight or locked off. When they're straight, you're hanging 'off the bone', but when locked off, you're straining your muscles and will quickly burn out, so focus on keeping the locked off time to a minimum. To do this, have a plan for each move before you do it. This means eyeing the next placement, bringing your feet up, locking off, placing your pick, then hanging back on to your arm. If you lock off and then try finding a placement, you'll waste a few more seconds, which, when multiplied over a pitch and the whole route, will result in tired arms. It's also worth doing lock-off training before the winter – done by simply locking off when doing pull-ups.

471. When you put your crampons on, always give the bails a tap with your hammer to check they're locked on properly.

472. Pull the buckle on your crampons round to the front inside of your ankle, so that you can do it up without being double-jointed.

473. With double-ring crampon buckles, pass the tape through once, and then pass it through a second time. You can also stop them freezing by giving the webbing a blast with WD-40 at the same time as you do your screws.

474. Try and see your crampons like you do your rock boots, making the most of all your points, especially the heel, as stepping all your weight on to the heel, or placing your crampon sideways, will take the strain off your calves.

475. Practise what Jeff Lowe described as 'hedging' – placing your inside edge on the ice, then rotating your ankle so the outside points engage as well.

476. When I'm getting close to a spot where I want to place a screw or want to rest before the crux, I will often chop away a small edge big enough for my crampons to fit sideways. Then I climb up on to it and stand in balance, giving my calves a breather.

477. If you're climbing thin ice where you can't place a pick deep enough to feel confident, then try cutting letterboxes in the ice, and place your pick sideways. These same letterboxes are then used as footholds, rather than kicking the thin ice.

478. On such thin ice climbs, you're probably going to be able to get rock gear in beyond stubby screws (I once climbed with someone who had a 2-centimetre screw for thin ice!), and in these situations you tend to need a big rack, as you don't know what you might find.

479. The key to getting rock gear on thin ice routes is understanding the rhythm of the rock; how its architecture and structure unfolds. Where are the cracks? Are corners blind? What about overlaps – do they have sweet spots where you can get cams to fit? If you can work out stuff like this, you'll be able to have a chance at chopping away sections of thin ice and getting solid rock pro.

480. When you've finished ice climbing, give all your hardware a quick blast with WD-40 before storing it away.

481. Don't worry about falling off – you're not allowed to, and, if you do, it will be so quick it'll be over in a flash, so why concern yourself? Instead, focus on climbing!

Old ring bolt on the Harlin route, Eiger.

The final pitch on the Lafaille route, Petit Dru.   **Photo**: Ian Parnell

Hot aches, the mixed climber's worst enemy!

005

MIXED (482–503)

"On a mixed route, you need to remember that you're more often than not on a line that in summer is a choss pile, and so loose blocks and killer flakes still abound. When pulling down on anything, take a cautious approach like you would on a loose sea cliff."

MIXED (482–503)

LEADING (482–494)

482. How many times have you set your pick into a lump of turf, a patch of ice or on to a flat hold but been too scared to move up on it? Probably quite a few. Also, how many times have you moved up on some crappy placement, only for your feet to cut loose and leave you fully hanging from said placements? Probably quite a few times as well. Free-climbing with hands and fingers allows you to judge in a split second if you can hold on, your fingertips sending back an 'OK' the moment they touch that crimp. Let's consider what happens when we no longer have that relationship between what we want to grasp and the brain. In aid climbing and winter climbing this link is broken by a necessary barrier (an axe, a peg, a skyhook), because what we want to grip is ungraspable (ice, snow or holds too small to hang from). In this situation, we can only go by our understanding of our physical world, the laws of physics and a big dose of trust and experience. A non-climber would trust an ice-axe pick hooked on to a climbing frame, because they know that if they pull, the pick won't be able to unhook itself. But if you asked them to climb a tree, they would be less confident, because although they understand that a tree is soft enough to take a pick, they are unsure how far the pick would have to go in to hold them. An ice-climber, on the other hand, builds up this knowledge, slowly at first: over-driving picks into ice or turf, and slowly defining in their head how much

depth is needed to hold. This is a combination of knowing how a pick works, and an understanding of the medium on which you're climbing. The same goes for mixed climbing: an axe torqued at 45 degrees will hold, whereas an axe torqued at 15 degrees won't. Slowly, we learn what is possible.

What I'm trying to say is that we don't learn what we can crimp with our fingers – we just know – but we don't know what we can climb using artificial means beyond the obvious, and instead we need to build this up over time. So this is where this tip comes in. What if you don't know? What if you're pushing your limit, say you're on Ben Nevis and you've got to climb ice only 2 inches thick, and you've only climbed névé 3 feet thick; or you're on a ledge and have to pull up on a flat hold and you've only hooked big stonking flakes before? In aid climbing, when you don't know what a piece of gear is capable of doing and the outcome of it coming out wouldn't be great, you bounce-test it, clipping in a sling and applying full body weight. This not only tells you that the gear is up to it, but it also tells your brain to relax and do the move. In winter climbing, this same approach can work really well when you're unsure or have a doubt in the placement. Unlike an aid climber who has two daisy chains to do this, you instead use your arms. To do this, place your tool and if you want to know if it's good, give it some good hard tugs. This actually takes some practice as you need to do it in such a way that if it does rip out you won't fall off. Also, go at it in the right frame of mind – think, 'I want to rip this pick out!', rather than, 'please don't rip out'. This technique is a great one for pushing your limit, but don't overuse it, as you'll climb much too slowly, and your arms will get very, very tired.

483. If you've never torqued a tool, then play around on buildings and walls, and get to grips with the concept that anything can be inserted into a space in one orientation, then locked there by changing that orientation.

The author on *The Vicar*, Northern Corries, Scotland.

484. Anything can be torqued in a crack and the trick is to be creative. This includes the pick, adze, hammer and shaft. Like a rock-climber who knows their rack, you need to view your axe like an aid rack, weighing up what bit will fit, where and how.

485. When you apply a torque, you have a narrow spectrum of effectiveness that goes from breaking the tool to the tool no longer applying enough force to stay locked in. In the middle of this spectrum is the 'perfect torque'. When you get that perfect torque, you must try and maintain it through the range of motion needed to get the next torque, which is basically the most important skill needed for hard winter climbing – well, in the UK anyway!

486. Tools are strong, but try to avoid redlining them when torquing, as picks do bend and break, axe heads snap off, and shafts shear.

487. One very handy technique when you get a pick wedged into a crack is to hammer it a little with your other tool, knocking it in that extra bit, giving you the confidence it won't rip. I've used this on a lot of climbs and it works really well for out-of-sight placements. (I remember using this on the crux of *Mitre Ridge* on the Garbh Choire of Beinn a'Bhuird a long time ago; I just placed my axe, gave it a few taps, and pulled up.) Of course, the trick is **not** to

hammer it to buggery, as you will make that move, only to come short as you find your axe is welded to the spot.

488. When hooking small, flat holds, it's vital that once you have a hook you're happy with, you do not change the angle or position of your pull or your pick. If you do, you stand a very good chance that it will rip. The best way to do this is to follow a great tip from Will Gadd, who said you should imagine that you've got a cup of coffee balanced on the head of your axe, and when you move you mustn't spill a drop.

MIXED (482–503)

489. A hook will also only work when pulling down, and so the higher you go, the more unstable it will become. Cranked tools with two high hand positions are designed to stay locked on, even when pulling from the top position, giving you that extra reach. Practise on a top rope, on a bridge or on a scrubby crag to see what your pick can do.

490. Once you can move comfortably on a hook, you'll find you have one more type of hold you can exploit.

491. Keep your picks sharp – which goes against the grain for Scottish mixed climbers – but a sharp pick will hold an edge much better as it will bite down and create a clear pivot point, meaning the tip won't walk off.

492. On a mixed route you need to remember that you're more often than not on a line that in summer is a choss pile, and so loose blocks and killer flakes still abound. When pulling down on anything, take a cautious approach like you would on a loose sea cliff. Sure, winter will freeze mud, grass and dirt, and will hold some things a little tighter, but a 200-kilogram block is still a 200-kilogram block.

493. Mixed belays tend to last longer than ice belays, perhaps for hours and hours, so make sure your belayer is prepared. This means wearing warm boots, a thick belay jacket (if you have more than one, then they can wear both), and having some food and drink handy.

494. If you get cold on the belay, do some air squats. Just squat down, and, as you do, point your arms out superman-style – stand and repeat. If that doesn't warm you up with all your winter kit on, then you must be dead.

GEAR (495–499)

495. Ice hooks are best not used on ice unless it is thin (place them sideways) or in tight spots (narrow bands of ice in off-width cracks), but they are great in turf, cracks and flakes. On rock, you should avoid hammering them into anything, as you'll never get them out again. If you feel they need hammering then just tap to seat them and a few blows will get the hook's teeth to bite. Try and get to grips with the shape of the hook and ask yourself if you should hammer it into the rock in the first place, as its length – being far longer than any peg – will always be a major pain in the arse to remove. This need to drive the peg all the way home is due to the peg's length, its lack of any taper and, because unlike an axe which will hook securely on the very tip of its pick, all current hook designs need to be set all the way in to avoid leverage.

496. A better alternative for a mixed peg, rather than an ice hook which is too long, is a large or medium beak. Both are lightweight and provide solid protection in some very barren places, and replace all other pegs on most racks.

497. On mixed terrain, you can stack your beaks together to fit Lost Arrow cracks, or stack them with nuts (orientate the nut upside down, so the hook is working against the nut's taper).

498. Large beaks can also be placed in horizontal cracks: just place and then lark's-foot a sling to tie off, or insert the wire from a nut through the hole in the beak's head.

499. To clean a stuck ice hook, try and 'funk' it out using a chain of krabs clipped from the hole in the head of the hook to the head of your axe. This may work as the peg is being pulled directly outwards, but it will require some hard yanks. Another option, and one that I find it works really well with such pegs, is to use a little bit of clever leverage. To do this, you hold a peg or another solid object just above the bottom eye of the hook to create a fulcrum, then hammer the bottom of the hook towards the rock (as if you were trying to get the bottom of the hook to stick in the crack). This should lever out the pick of the hook, even when it's really embedded in the rock. You can adjust your fulcrum point to suit the hook style and its depth.

FOOTWORK (500–503)

500. On a mixed route, unlike a rock route in rock boots, there is less room for error as the connection between you and your foothold is dulled by many layers of rubber, steel, plastic and wool, not to mention frozen toes and feet that are hidden by lots of clothing and a tangled rack. With a rock boot you have a much higher degree of leeway and creep. In most cases, when your feet pop, you know it already. With crampons this isn't the case and very often your foot has little room to move before it skates, meaning when you place it, try and keep it still.

501. Exploit more than just your front points. If you're about to start a long search for some gear, try using your heel instead of your toes to take your weight.

502. The most important lesson to learn is to not undermine your feet – the major engine of your ascent – by focusing too much on your arms. By this I mean that the winter climber focuses on his or her tools; after all they are right in front of your face. What we do is look for a tool placement, set our feet, pull with the axes and push with the feet. Yet very often we have good footholds, but nothing for our axes to pull on. Worse still is pulling on crap placements when we have stonking footholds that we could climb in balance, if not for the fact we're pulling on crap. What I'm saying is that sometimes you're better off dropping your tools (hook them on your shoulder) and just use your feet, using balance and pressing your hands to make the move. Many instructors use this approach with novice ice climbers, making them climb without tools at all, but it's a skill we can all learn from for our own mixed adventures.

503. A lot of climbers talk about having a sensitive boot, and much is made of this in boot ads, but personally I'm more interested in how solid and how warm I feel in my boots. This means I tend to wear big boots like Sportiva Spantiks as I like being able to stand on a small hold for a long time. Some people take this to extremes and actually wear ski mountaineering boots. Also, no one climbs well when their toes are frozen. The one exception to this, and perhaps where this has come from, is super-athletic winter climbing, where you're mainly dangling from your axes on steep ground. Here, weight is crucial, but on slabs and faces, being able to stand your ground is way more important.

Calum Muskett approaching the north face of the Matterhorn.

The author on the first winter ascent of Aguja Guillaumet, Patagonia.

006

MOUNTAIN (504–802)

"For time over distance, add 30 seconds for every 10-metre contour."

CREVASSES (504–514)

504. You need to have rock-solid crevasse rescue skills and experience before you even get to any ice. This means going down to the climbing wall or local crag and spending a day practising self-rescue – prusiking and hauling other people out.

505. When travelling across glaciers, everyone should have two prusik loops (1.5 metres of 5-millimetre and 2.5 metres of 5-millimetre), two mechanical ascenders (Petzl Tibloc), an ice screw (good quality and 17-centimetre or 22-centimetre), a 120-centimetre sling, several locking karabiners and a penknife. If you're only a two-person team, you should double the slings and screws, but in larger teams carry a second group kit and share carrying between two climbers. This would be one extra screw, two 60-centimetre slings, one 120-centimetre sling and a locking pulley like a Petzl Micro Traxion. But remember this gear is worthless if you don't know how to use it.

506. Communication is vital in any rescue and even more so when someone is down a hole, as it can be almost impossible to hear anything from either end of the rope. By training together, you will know what the other person will do, and if there are three people in the team, then someone should crawl forward to communicate between the climber and the rescuer.

507. If you find yourself down a slot, then unless you can climb out easily, you should make sure you're not going to get hypothermia; your body temperature will drop rapidly, especially if you were up on the surface in your base layers during the midday heat. For this reason, it's worth having your belay jacket in the top of your pack.

508. Don't just start hauling up the fallen climber unless you know they need pulling up. The ideal scenario is that they climb out, followed by prusiking out (less ideal), then assisted prusiking, and, lastly, full-on hauling.

509. Make all training as close to reality as possible. Go out on a cold dark night and wear the kit you will be wearing, including mitts, and begin with just hanging in space (you can do this from a tree) in full kit, including crampons, ski poles and pack. You will soon realise that there's a huge difference between reading about technique in a book and applying it in real-world situations.

510. Don't take coils on a glacier, and belay each other in and out from safe areas.

511. All packs need to have a leash attached to their haul loop with a karabiner attached (clip this into the bottom area of the rucksack strap so you can find it). If you find yourself down a hole, you'll want to take off your sack to make climbing easier and to get through tight spots.

512. Every member of the rope should be skilled enough to rescue any other member – even *all* other members. This means that they carry the basic equipment to carry out a rescue, or have the ability to call for help; it is not good planning to have the most experienced climber disappear down a slot with all the kit and the phone.

513. Crevasses, narrow slots and holes can form anywhere. They can be caused by both glacial movement, and by boulders melting down into the ice or watercourses during a big melt. Consequently, you should always be on your guard, and unless you're standing on solid rock or the balcony of an Alpine hut then keep on your toes.

514. Most crevasses are not *Touching the Void*-style abysses where you end up hanging in space, but a tight helter-skelter that can twist and break limbs, with snow falling down that will bury you alive, and kill you before you can be pulled out. If you just get stuck in the slot, your body heat will begin to melt the ice walls, slowly trapping you deeper and deeper until hypothermia sets in. Horrible thought. Keep that in mind when you're next on a glacier and keep your team tight and on the ball.

CLOTHING, BOOTS AND EQUIPMENT (515–526)

515. Boots coming undone can be either an annoyance or highly dangerous if you're on steep ice, so it's worth tying a solid knot. The problem with tying multiple bow knots is that when your laces become frozen, they can be hard to undo. There are many variations that work better, such as when you make the first part of the knot (crossing laces, then passing one under the other) you wrap the other lace twice around the first, as this locks the knot much tighter. My own favourite (I couldn't tie my shoelaces until I was about twelve years old) is to just tie a reef knot – simple! This only works on tubular laces and not flat laces. To untie, just take one lace and yank it backwards and forwards against the other side of the knot, and this will loosen up the knot so it can be pulled apart. Since this knot needs short laces, you can cut them so they're neat.

516. Write your name on your inner and outer boots, or mark them so they can't be mixed up in drying rooms or with your mates' boots. If you're super-clumsy then add your address too.

517. A clean pair of socks is almost as good as a complete change of clothing, and when you're feeling smelly, remember that Fridtjof Nansen wore the same underwear for over a year, turning it inside out for a treat on Christmas Day.

518. Make sure your boots (inner and outer) have a clip-in cord attached that is well tied and secure, so you can clip off your boots at bivvies. I tend to add a long loop to the back of my inner boots to make it easier to pull them on in my sleeping bag. The left one is tied with two single fisherman's knots, while the right one is tied with a double, so I can tell which is which when they're stuffed down the bottom of my sleeping bag.

519. The trick to staying warm in the mountains is to stay cool, which translates as staying dry. Most people wear too many clothes at the start of the day, when they will do the most work in the approach, and then end up cold the rest of the day as their clothes are saturated. It's better to start a little cold and get warm on the approach, then add clothes when standing around or during lower levels of activity (such as climbing) once you get to the climb.

520. Get some good-quality electronic scales to weigh your gear, and write the weight on all your clothing, sleeping bags, rucksacks and heavy kit in permanent marker, so you can work out whether to take it or leave it when you're at base camp.

MOUNTAIN (504–802)

521. Don't wear a shell unless it's raining, as no matter how breathable it is, it won't be breathable enough. Carry a light shell ($\approx$ 200 grams) and only wear it when it's totally needed. Instead, wear a super-breathable Pertex top with a hood, which when worn over just a base layer will provide all the protection you will need in almost any situation when moving.

522. Adjust your body temperature by working with your hand wear, headwear and venting – putting on and taking off hats and mitts, and rolling up sleeves, unzipping tops, and tweaking what you're wearing to limit your perspiration.

523. Good training for how to dress well in the mountains is winter running, or going out in crap weather. Moving fast in just your shorts, a T-shirt and a windproof in such weather will give you confidence in your body, and help you understand the true meaning of a microclimate.

524. By far the best base layer for mountain use is the Norwegian mesh underwear most commonly found in the form of Brynje Super Thermo. Although it looks like something your grandfather would wear.

525. Your speed is the accelerator and decelerator of your comfort: if you get too hot, slow down, and if you get too cold, speed up. If you're climbing with people less fit than you, then wear more clothes.

526. Taking a spare base layer to change into once you reach your climb is a good idea, and if you're super sweaty, or the approach is very hard, then consider a spare pair of socks as well.

SLEEPING BAGS AND MATS (527–545)

527. If you're in a wet environment or cooking inside a confined space, try to avoid getting your sleeping bag out until you've finished. This will stop moisture entering your bag, or wetting the outside of it.

528. If it's super cold and you've made it into a tent and have the stove on, the air temperature will quickly rise to something a little more than normal. Resist the temptation to pull out your sleeping bag for a while and instead leave it in a waterproof bag, as exposing a super-cooled sleeping bag will cause any moisture to condense on it.

529. I'm a big fan of sleeping bags with a little zipper pocket in the hood or on the Velcro tab that locates the hood. Most people don't know what this is for, and assume it's for your condoms – but no, it's meant for your watch. If you leave your watch out in the cold, it may stop working, and if you leave it on your wrist, you will probably not hear the alarm if it's buried deep in that super-warm bag. If your bag doesn't have a pocket then sew one on (a little pocket of fleece sewn on to the edge of the hood works, or attach the watch to the draw cord).

530. Nine times out of ten, when you wake up in the morning, the Velcro tab designed to hold your neck baffle closed will be undone. The problem is the Velcro is usually too light to do the job, but if it's cold, having it come undone can mean you lose a lot of warmth. Beef this up by adding more Velcro, ideally two pieces that lock down on either side of a third piece (with the Velcro sewn on both sides).

531. When you go to sleep, you will probably have quite a lot of warmth to spare in your body, coming primarily from your dinner but also from the movement of sorting out your sleeping bag and mat. This heat will slowly dissipate during the night, so it's vital to hold on to as much as possible, because if you wake up cold at 2 a.m. you're going to have a hard time generating more heat. Lock down your bag so no heat can escape, and keep it locked down. If you take off clothes then consider lying on top of them, or having them in your bag so you can get the last bits of heat from them (they will also be warm in the morning).

532. If you have damp shells, then lying on top of them (under a bivvy bag) can dry them overnight, or you can just lay them over your bivvy bag. Laying an item over your bag, even something thin like a waterproof jacket, can add around 5 °C of insulation to that area of the bag.

533. Having a pillow will improve your sleep – Joe Tasker famously always carried one on his routes. You can fashion a pillow by making a stuff sack out of thin polyester fleece on one side and Pertex on the other, and put gear inside to form a pillow; maybe your inner boots and your mitts. By storing items under your sleeping bag, you prevent them from freezing as well.

534. Always tie a clip-in loop to any mat you use, as they can easily be lost when sorting out a tight bivvy, or just dropped (a foam mat is hard to hold on to when wearing mitts). With a foam mat, just puncture the corner and thread with cord. With an inflatable mat, reinforce the edge with duct tape wrapped around a loop of cord.

535. If you use a long-enough bungee cord as your clip-in loop, it can double up as a way of keeping your mat rolled up.

536. An inflatable mat is obviously very fragile in an environment full of sharp things, so try and place it in your sack where it has the best chance of survival. This is usually down the back of the pack, away from sharp objects (tools and crampons) that may pierce the body of the pack. Just get all the air out, then fold it in half down the middle, then fold it in half in the other direction. With a three-quarter-length mat, you should now have an oblong that will slip into the back of the pack (leave the clip-in loop at the top edge so you can clip off the mat as soon as you pull it out).

537. Have a 'punctured mat' strategy worked out. Do you have a repair kit? Can you use your pack as insulation? On a winter route, you can rest your heels on your inner boots, your ass on your rucksack, and fold up the punctured mat for your shoulders. And lie on the rope as well.

538. For big, multi-week trips, take both an inflatable mat and a foam mat – this gives you comfort and redundancy. Although, personally, I would just take two foam mats, as this takes any stress out of a trip; someone always has a slow puncture, and lying there at 2 a.m. while they pump up their mat will give you a self-satisfied glow.

539. There is an ongoing debate about whether it is a good idea to wear all your clothes or take them off when sleeping in a bag that's not quite warm enough. I think you should always take off anything that's damp (shell, softshells and socks) and either put on a dry replacement, or dry that body part. If your base layer and fleece are dry then keep them on, but avoid anything that will trap moisture (most membrane base softshells do). Also avoid wearing anything that is super bulky inside the bag, as this can reduce the loft of your bag. The classic mistake is to wear your belay jacket in your bag, but leave your legs exposed to the cold. Ideally you need to keep all your body warm, as having cold feet, or legs, will just rob what heat you have. Instead I would take off my fleece and lay that over my legs (you can stick your feet in the arms), and lay the belay jacket over my body (arms pulled in) so I was getting the maximum benefit of its insulation (i.e. no lying on half of it).

540. If you want to save weight on a route you believe you can climb in a single push, then consider taking just a single sleeping bag and using it like a blanket over both climbers. The one downside is that you won't be able to use a bivvy bag, but if you carry a lightweight tent such as a Black Diamond Firstlight, you can use this as a two-person bivvy bag – or, better still, as a tent!

541. Take all sleeping bag temperature ratings with a large pinch of salt, as your comfort is based on far more factors than just how much trapped air you'll have in your bag. These factors include how tired you are, how warm/cold you are on entering the bag, your hydration, hunger levels, and so on. The bottom line is: being comfortable takes work and planning.

542. In super-cold temperatures, breathing cold air will lower your body temperature, plus such cold temperatures may force you to breathe inside your bag. This will raise the temperature of the air going into your lungs, but it will also raise the amount of moisture inside your sleeping bag. Using a face mask such as a ColdAvenger, where the warm air is trapped, will allow you to sleep warmer and also protect your face while sleeping.

543. Whenever you take a leak in your piss bottle, try and drink the same amount of liquid from your water bottle – just don't get them mixed up!

544. If your down sleeping bag gets wet, it will still provide some warmth, and it may be possible to dry it out. To do this, separate out the down clumps as much as possible with your fingers and spread them over the top of the bag (because they are heavy they will want to migrate down the sides). Now sleep in the bag with extra insulation, such as a fleece and a belay jacket, over the top of the bag. This will help push the moisture up out of the down. It's easier to dry out a synthetic bag this way – and a synthetic bag is also the best way to avoid moisture getting into your bag in the first place.

545. If you're bringing a full Nalgene bottle into your sleeping bag anyway, then if you boil the water first it will raise the temperature of your bag greatly, helping to kick-start the bag's insulation. Place it between your legs as this is where your two major arteries run, and this should warm you up pretty well.

The author on the *Supercanaleta*, Fitz Roy, Patagonia.

Digging out tents after a winter storm, Norway.

MOUNTAIN BIVVIES (546–555)

546. Summer nights are short and tend not to be too cold, so you can get away with a thin sleeping bag, or just a duvet if you're hard. If you want to keep it light just wear a warm duvet and carry some belay pants and a bivvy bag. You can also stand in your pack, boil some water for your Nalgene and stick it between your legs, and just aim for a kip of a few hours. And stop late and start early.

547. When setting up a belay on a ledge, make a handline between a solid belay and a second belay, one at each end – you can clip off all your kit, and yourself, along the line.

548. If you want to remain tight to a belay but also want to be able to move, tie into the rope with enough slack to move anywhere on the bivvy, then adjust the length with a prusik loop or a mini ascender.

549. On a sitting bivvy, try and use something to lean sideways on, such as a rucksack, or chop back a snow ledge so you can recline as much as possible.

550. A sitting bivvy is always a little grim and you'll end up with a sore arse, but if you have to do it for a few days, you'll get used to it. Just remember: it's better than standing!

551. Never sleep in your inner boots as your socks won't dry and your feet will freeze the following morning. Multiple days without taking off your boots will lead to trench foot (basically your feet will start dying).

552. You should always sleep with your inner boots, but they can take up quite a bit of room in your bag. The main section of the boot that needs drying is the insole, so take this out and stick it in your layers, then push one boot into the other, and tie them together so they stay locked. Now just place the two boots between your legs.

553. A hammock can make a hard bivvy a lot less hard. You can lean into it, or place it below your feet so you can all support your feet on it. A string hammock is probably the best style for climbing, as it can be clipped in a million different ways to tweak it for whatever you need it to do.

554. If you're on a rocky ledge strewn with rocks and you have the time, try terracing it by laying stones to make a flat platform to sleep on, and, once that's done, try making a rough dry-stone wall. This may sound like a lot of work, but if you don't have good bivvy kit then it'll keep you warm, and having a wall will keep you warmer than nothing.

555. To dry damp socks and gloves, put them next to your skin inside your sleeping bag – stick them on your stomach, under your armpits or between your legs.

NAVIGATION AND STORM TACTICS (556–600)

556. The red end of the compass needle points north – and it's not red because it points to the hot south!

557. You won't get good at navigation, or even grasp the very basics of navigation, without practice, so go out and learn how to get from A to B. Try the 'box' method to learn the basics: go to a field, stick your rucksack down, walk 100 metres, take a bearing at 90 degrees and walk for 100 metres, take another bearing at 90 degrees, walk 100 metres, and one more time. Are you back at your rucksack?

558. Basic navigation on a sunny day in Snowdonia, where a mistake will only be embarrassing, is very different to finding your way off a Scottish summit at night and in a storm, where you know one mistake could kill you. Learn the basics, and then make life harder for yourself. Just a few hours out at night will help sharpen up your skills; throw in bad weather as well and you'll soon be a pro.

559. Trust your map and compass, not your gut feeling or intuition; the former will always be right, the latter – when overruling the former – will always be wrong.

560. Don't let over-optimism, or a willingness to adapt reality to what you want to happen, lead you astray. If you get lost and suddenly think that somehow you've covered 50 kilometres in an hour, then, unless you've dropped through a wormhole, you're probably wrong.

561. When navigating, always keep a level head and never make rash judgements.

562. If you're lost, take your time to work out where you are. Orientate the map correctly and take a long look at both your map and compass until you think you know where you are.

563. Don't let animal tracks fool you into thinking you are on a path – they will generally be narrower and go somewhere you don't want to go.

564. If you're lost, try to stay high until you're either sure you know the way down, or you think you're going to die from exposure. Dropping down to a remote valley when exhausted, and having to climb back up, or simply waiting to get rescued, is not good.

565. When navigating at night, don't forget to use the moon and the stars as navigational aids, with the North Star (Polaris) being the obvious one to look for. Having a working knowledge of the stars is both useful and fun.

566. When doing complex micro-navigation in the dark, it is a good idea to cover your head torch every now and then to check the landscape, as you will be able to see major outlines and features that would be otherwise invisible with the head torch beam on.

567. If you're trying to pick up tracks, stay on tracks or look for footprints in the dark, then carry your head torch in your hands, not strapped to your head, especially if it's foggy, snowing or raining. Having it low will allow the beam to pick up more shadows, detail and texture.

568. Try to keep to one scale of map, with 1:50,000 being simpler and less detailed than 1:25,000, which is far more complex. If you switch from one to the other, it will take a while to get to grips with distance and time.

569. Night-time navigation is not directly helped by people having reflective tape on their gear, but it comes in very handy. Make sure everyone has reflective tape on the front and back: a patch on the shoulder strap, and one on the back of the head (glue or sew it on to the back of your head torch). This comes in very handy if walking in line on a bearing, as it allows the person at the rear in a three-person team to shout out if the person at the front is straying off the bearing. It also aids in rescue situations.

570. Time over distance is good for planning, or for using with dead reckoning to work out where you should be (an average person walks 100 metres in 90 seconds, 1 kilometre in 15 minutes). But for micro-navigation – the stuff that gets you back in a whiteout – you need to use pace. A pace is two steps, so every time your right foot moves it is one pace. On flat ground, you will cover 100 metres in around 65 paces, but it's worth measuring this in a test environment first, such as a school field, not with the weather battering your face with so much force you feel like your eyes are bleeding.

571. Your pace will be affected by the steepness of the slope (95 paces for steep terrain), the terrain (75 paces for medium scree), snow depth (120 paces), darkness (75 paces), mist and wind.

572. If you just need rudimentary calculations of distance then don't sweat it too much, but if you're doing micro-navigation, then treat it as seriously as if you've been asked to walk through a minefield. Count it out.

573. For time over distance, add 30 seconds for every 10-metre contour.

574. You can check out your pace and timing by just walking a rope length. If you have a 60-metre rope, walk it and time yourself and count your paces (count each time you step with your right foot). Now divide this by 60 and multiply that number by 100 for your 100-metre time – make a note of it (write it on your compass and inside your map case in permanent marker. By the time it wears off you'll know it anyway.).

575. If you have a bad memory, make a small, credit-card-sized pace card with your pace count over different terrain types, and tape this inside your map case.

576. Make a route card the night before you go into an area or into conditions where you think things might be tricky. Work out the legs in and out, and not the waypoints, noting bearings, altitude, distance and expected times. Put this in your map case facing outwards so you can check it.

577. Calculate times in minutes and use a stopwatch to check progress, making adjustments for weather and terrain, but remembering to pause it when you stop moving.

578. Make a pace counter and attach it to your rucksack straps. Take a length of 3-millimetre cord and tie a solid figure-of-eight knot in the end. Now slide nine small cord locks on to it, and, 20 centimetres above the last one (with all of them pushed to the end), tie a knot in the cord to stop the cord locks from sliding off, and then add four more cord locks. These four will be your 1-kilometre markers. Finish with a second figure-of-eight. To measure distance, push one of your nine cord locks down for each 100 metres, and when you hit the 1-kilometre mark, push a 1-kilometre cord lock up and push all the 100-metre cord locks down and begin again. At your 5-kilometre mark, push all cord locks down and start again.

579. If you're pace counting, then shout out each 100 metres as you get to them, so that if you forget you're counting then someone else will notice. It will also be recorded in your hearing (auditory) memory.

580. If you top out and really need to be sure you've nailed your distance calculations, you can always just 'pitch it', with one person walking on a bearing for one rope length (around 58 metres), then bringing the second forward, and repeating. This may sound like a funny thing to do, but even if you're laughing now, you may not be when you top out and can't even see the crag you're standing on.

581. Remember if you're on skis or wearing snowshoes your pacing will be different.

582. The night before you go on the hill, check the map for backup options for if you can't carry out your planned descent, so you have the basics of an alternative plan worked out.

583. Use your watch so you can judge both your movement over the terrain and also time lost when talking or trying to work out where the hell you are.

584. An altimeter watch is a great bit of kit for checking where you are. Just remember to set it to the correct height at the start of the day, or throughout the day when you come to locations of known altitude if the pressure is changing due to the weather.

585. Make sure your watch is visible, as having it hidden under a closed cuff and mitts is not good. Get a system where you can put it over your layers, or wear it on your rucksack strap.

586. A change in temperature can also affect your altimeter, so that's another good reason to keep it out from underneath sweaty layers.

587. If your life depends on getting off with a map and a compass, don't just have one map and compass, but have two people navigating at the same time, one being the prime leader, and the other double-checking.

588. The majority of difficult navigation legs are relatively short, so staying focused should be fine, but rotate the person up front if the leg goes on for more than 15 minutes (or every 500 metres if things are particularly tough).

589. If you're navigating around a big cliff section in a white-out, stay tied in with enough rope out to stop the leader falling, and pay close attention to ensure you're not walking in line along a cornice.

590. When out front in a white-out close to big cliffs, use pace counting and every 10 paces make a snowball and throw it forwards. Walk to it then throw it again.

591. Judging slope angle in a white-out can be hard, and using a ski pole held out in front of you can help. Just work out where it will be when held out in front of you on the flat, and then work from that. You can also throw snowballs and see where they are.

592. In really terrible conditions, if you're scared of getting lost and not finding the route off, consider the feasibility of just going back down the route you came up.

593. If you want to have a backup plan of going back down the route, but would like to try getting off by walking first, then make a snow cairn at the top-out point, as big as you can, then, staying roped together, make another one at each rope length. To find your way back, you know that if you find a cairn the next one will be one rope length away.

594. If you have a GPS, then make sure you know how to use it and have a spare set of batteries in a Ziploc bag.

595. Ensure your compass is attached to you somehow, as it can be hard to find when dropped in a snowdrift.

596. If you use a waterproof map, still use a waterproof map case but write important information such as leg distances and bearings on the map with a non-permanent marker.

597. Always using a map case is a good idea, because in really shocking weather you will need to have it attached to you (I know of at least one team who had to be rescued when their map blew away). Attach a piece of bungee cord to a wiregate karabiner and clip this off to your rucksack strap, and stuff the map under your shoulder strap so you can see the relevant area of the map when you look down.

598. If you're doing micro-navigation (you're moving through a complex area where you need to switch direction a few times in a few hundred metres), then keep your thumb over the map, and keep checking distance and bearing every few minutes.

599. If you have a big team, then give everyone a number, and get them to shout out their number one at a time to check everyone is accounted for. Make one person the leader ('one'), so when they shout 'one!', everyone answers ('two!', 'three!', etc.). If you're in a big storm, this will help people to feel part of the group and not isolated.

600. When navigation is tough and every cell of your body is screaming for you to just 'get out of here' – take a deep breath and follow the *Kama Sutra*: 'whatever you're doing, do it at half the speed'.

Where do we start?

MOUNTAIN (504–802)

REPAIR KIT (601–633)

601. If you're on any kind of route, it's a good idea to carry a kit to make repairs. This kit can range from a needle and a thread for sewing up rips and worn gloves, to a kit so extensive you could probably make your own kit from scratch. The following are items that you may need, and on a big, remote trip I'd take all of it.

602. Always carry a small selection of good-quality needles. Don't get them from the supermarket; go for good-quality sailing needles designed for repairing sail, and which are good for heavy-duty work.

603. Use good-quality bonded polyester thread and either wrap it around a cut-down pencil, or a sewing machine bobbin (secure with an elastic band). You can also use an old credit card, cutting a section out of two sides, then wrap the thread around this. This way you will get a flat bobbin. The credit card may also come in handy, unless it's an American Express, which is good for nothing at all.

604. Take along some heavy-duty sail repair thread for heavy-duty jobs. This is usually waxed and is high strength, but it needs heavy-duty needles and perhaps something strong to push the needle through (use this to repair rucksack straps).

605. Carry a couple of sewing needle threaders, which weigh nothing but are lifesavers when it comes to threading a bloody needle while wearing gloves.

606. Take a single bodkin pin, a tool designed to be threaded through seams to get elastic or cord around a hem, which can come in handy for many other things, such as getting a camel to fit through something very small.

607. Heavy-duty and lightweight safety pins (sizes 1, 2 and 3).

608. Don't forget a thimble, which will protect your delicate fingers, and can also be used to drink whisky from if you want to give the impression that you're a Viking giant.

609. Ten pins with plastic heads (inserted into a patch of fleece), vital for joining fabrics when sewing them back together. Stick them into a piece of heavy-duty fabric along with your other needles.

610. Three metres of 1-millimetre kite Dyneema.

611. Three metres of 2-millimetre Dyneema cord for makeshift repairs of tents, cams and sacks.

612. Thirty metres of Paracord. Cheaper than Perlon and very good for millions of jobs, such as spare shoelaces (cut it down though, as 30-metre shoe laces are ostentatious), washing and food lines, and setting up a tarp.

613. Two metres of 4-millimetre bungee cord.

614. Thirty centimetres of 25-millimetre Velcro (male and female).

615. Three buttons. Why would you need a button in this day and age? Well, they can be quite handy if your zipper breaks apart on your tent, sleeping bag or jacket, plus you can play 'button football' if you get desperate.

616. Mini sewing snips.

617. Spare lighter. Lighters are crap, but when you don't have a spare, something always happens to make you wish you had one.

618. One small nut and bolt with washer (3-millimetre by 20-millimetre).

619. A few metres of duct tape wound around a pencil or a credit card.

620. A small waterproof notebook. Handy for writing notes, drawing maps, topos, or just working out how much stuff you've lost after a big trip! You can also make a chess set out of one if things get desperate.

621. Superglue. Keep it inside two plastic bags in case it explodes.

622. Spare battery for your watch. A dead watch wouldn't be great thing to have on any alpine trip where you need to wake up early.

623. Ten alloy swages. These have loads of uses and can be crimped with a multi-tool or just shaped with a hammer.

624. One metre of copper wire. This can be used to repair all sorts of things, and can even be used for heavy-duty sewing. I've used mine to make a new trigger for a cam, and to hold a broken stove burner head on to the stove.

625. A 15-millimetre Fastex buckle. This can come in handy if someone loses a crampon strap, or if a chest buckle gets broken.

626. One metre of 15-millimetre nylon webbing for the buckle.

627. One 15-millimetre ladderlock buckle.

628. Three freezer bag clips. These have all sorts of odd uses; in fact you'll soon wish you had more. Their main uses are for keeping bags of sugar, milk, foot powder etc. closed, but they can also be used to repair tents.

629. Roll of Spinnaker or Mylar tape to repair tents and clothing. This can be sewn or stuck into place.

630. Plastic cable ties (big and small). Buy good quality ties that won't break in the cold, and get a good selection of sizes. You can join many cables together to make long ones.

631. Metal cable ties (small). More expensive, but also more robust and they won't melt, so more useful for mending stoves and pans.

632. Two medium-sized jubilee clips (type of clamp). Another little piece of hardware that can come in handy for some unknown task, such as mending a ski or tent pole.

633. Plastic business card box. A tiny box that's invaluable for keeping all the tiny bits of your repair kit in one place.

Crevasse bivvy in Patagonia.   **Photo**: Ian Parnell

SNOW SHELTERS (634–653)

634. Read up about different types of snow shelters on the internet, and watch videos on YouTube, but remember that most of this information is aimed at North American backwoods use, and these shelters are perhaps overbuilt for climbers, who generally need to dig a snow hole which they will only use once.

635. If you don't have any snow building tools then you'll have to make the most of your adze. Modern leashless axes tend to be far inferior to straight alpine axes, and often using the pick works best, drawing and chopping the compacted snow.

636. If you don't have a shovel, you can use the plastic back frame from your rucksack, along with your axe, to drag the spoil away.

637. The ideal tools for digging a mountaineering snow hole are a good-quality shovel, with a handle that telescopes to short or full length (one for lightweight hole building or two for luxury building), and an avalanche probe to check snow depth before you start digging (you can use lengths of bamboo taped together). All of these things can be improvised.

638. If you have an alloy stake in your pack, you can use it to cut out blocks in soft snow.

639. When digging a snow hole, you will get very hot and very wet, so strip down and wear your waterproofs. Books always mention it, but until you dig a snow hole for yourself you won't believe it.

640. Always follow the 100/20 per cent rule: when you think it's big enough, make it 20 per cent bigger, because once you're inside with all your kit, you won't want to move again.

641. If there's two of you, then kneel on a foam mat and push snow between your legs, while your mate shovels that spoil away. Alternatively, have the second person pull the mat away every few minutes and dump the snow, sort of like a closed-cell conveyor belt.

642. When digging an emergency snow hole, make it just big enough so that you can sit up and sleep head to toe. Building it any bigger is a waste of energy if it's only going to be of short-term use.

643. Follow the basic rules of snow hole building: keep a small vent (using a ski pole) so oxygen can flow in, and make the walls smooth so you don't get drips.

644. Burning a candle will warm up the snow hole and also give you some indication of oxygen levels.

645. If you want to check oxygen levels, try sparking up your lighter. If it doesn't produce a flame you may have a problem, so get some venting.

646. If you have a tarp, then a quicker method of making a snow shelter is to dig a hole (cave) big enough for the team (head to toe), making it deep enough to sit up in with plenty of room, then string out your tarp over the hole, securing its edges with axes, ski poles or dead pegs (ice screws buried sideways). If you have skis then these should be placed over the top of the hole as well before putting over the tarp. Now shovel a thin layer of snow over the tarp to stop it flapping, and add some insulation. Lastly, dig down and in. You will get some condensation from the tarp, meaning this is best used for one or two nights, but it can be dug pretty fast.

647. Cut a deep hole inside the entrance to your snow hole. This well will trap cold air, make it easier to step into the snow hole, and give the person who is cooking somewhere to sit comfortably.

648. Learn to dig a snow trench by digging a shoulder-width, waist-deep trench around 10 feet long. Now cut off blocks of snow and, leaning one against another, make a roof of blocks along the length, shovelling snow over the edges and filling in the gaps with soft snow and more blocks. You will slide in from one end, and this end can be protected by a snow wall to stop snow blowing in if the wind changes (like a tunnel tent, you want the closed end facing the wind). Again make a well at one end to trap cold air. You can sleep head to head inside, or cut away the sidewalls a little so you can sleep side by side. The ideal tools for making one of these shelters are a shovel and snow saw. How effective are these shelters? Well, I know a few people who have survived in them up on Denali in winter, where the temperature can get down to -50 °C!

649. If you know you will be spending more than one or two days in a snow hole, you should plan to make it more habitable. Begin by enlarging the snow hole so you don't touch the side walls, and elevate the sleeping area. (Or dig a trench along the front edge of the inside, and cut back into the snowpack to create an area where you can stand, sit more comfortably, and that also acts as a cold air trap.)

650. Multiple days or a week living in a snow hole can be fun or totally squalid – the right kit can make the difference. Spending all your time in your sleeping bag isn't healthy, so even in bad weather, try and do something productive. Having shelves cut into the walls makes it easier to keep your home ship-shape, and if you have synthetic belay pants and booties, you can get out of your bags and play cards, chat, or engage in naked wrestling (a good way to offset sexual frustration).

651. I've spent many weeks in snow holes, and months in total, and by far the most important item you need, apart from a good shovel, is a good book – or several!

652. Having a plastic groundsheet inside a snow hole can make life drier, as you can keep your living area free of snow and ice and your gear dry – snow and ice will always be wet in a snow shelter, which is why these shelters work: they keep the air, you and your gear above freezing temperatures.

653. If you're considering a life of alpine or expedition climbing then spend a day practising digging snow shelters, as often, when you end up digging your first real one, conditions will be far from ideal.

FOOD (654–690)

654. If you're forced to eat in 'difficult' spots, such as on a cramped ledge or a sitting bivvy, then it's vital to keep your food and cooking arrangements as simple as possible. The US Army used to give their soldiers MRE (Meal, Ready-to-Eat) pouches that contained a whole meal designed to fulfil their daily calorie requirements. The problem was that in action, fighting in the hills of Afghanistan, they proved far too heavy or bulky, plus soldiers didn't have the time or inclination to cook them up (MRE pouches came with a heating pouch that you heated by adding water). This meant that the soldiers started leaving food behind or just chucking away all the heavy crap (a high percentage of the weight was packaging), just taking food they could eat on the move. As a result, a pared-down meal called FSR – First Strike Ration – was developed that contained 2,900 calories (14% protein, 34% fat, 52% carbohydrate) to be consumed within three days. After that, the soldier would have to switch to MREs or else see a drop in performance. What's this got to do with climbing? Well, a soldier operates in the same kind of world as a mountaineer or an alpinist – carrying heavy shit, moving over distance, camping out in hostile environments – and all the while having to maintain optimum performance. The FSR contains a sandwich (wrap), two packets of drink mix, two energy bars, one breakfast bar, two packets of beef jerky, nut/trail mix, plus toilet roll, matches, salt and moisturising towels. To me, this sounds like a great starting point for alpine food on one- or two-day routes.

655. My 'Alpine FSR' would be made up in day (Ziploc) bags for each person, so they can be handed out before the climb, and would comprise:

- one large muesli bar (breakfast)
- one small packet of peanuts (mid-morning snack)
- two small beef jerky sticks (lunch, snack or dinner)
- two small (triangle-style) cheese portions (lunch, snack or dinner)
- one small packet of oatcakes (lunch, snack or dinner)
- one mini packet of butter (for oatcakes)
- one sachet of mayonnaise (lunch, snack or dinner)
- one packet of couscous or one bagel/wrap with cream cheese if you're climbing in a push (dinner)
- one cup of soup (dinner)
- two energy gels
- two teabags
- one sachet of sports drink
- one mini packet of chewy sweets
- a toilet roll.

Take a small onion, a clove or two of garlic, salt and pepper, baby tomatoes or anything that will spice up your food.

656. It took me many years to understand that eating every four hours was the best way to maintain performance and avoid hitting a wall. Taking breakfast at 5 a.m. and then eating nothing until a packet of noodles at 10 p.m. is not conducive to good sports performance.

657. Following the FSR model, eat a muesli-style bar for breakfast as you drink your morning coffee or tea. You can do this inside your sleeping bag or while getting sorted.

658. Make a habit of saving the last few bites of any bar and sticking it in your pocket to be eaten two hours later. This top-up should help maintain your energy levels (remember to eat every four hours).

659. If you want something more traditional, then go for instant porridge that you buy in those little bags – just add water. If you have no water then you can eat this raw, or add it to other meals, leaving it for a few minutes to absorb the water.

660. Jelly sweets such as Haribo are good both for morale and for keeping your energy levels up when working hard. Don't eat too many as they're bad for your teeth.

661. Sweets are also great mixed with snow when you're out of water. Just stick some snow in your mouth as you suck on the sweets, it will take the edge off your thirst.

662. If you're out of water and you need to eat snow, try eating ice instead, as you get more water from ice. Always be careful of stones or dirt held in the ice, as this could chip your teeth, or give you an upset stomach if swallowed.

663. Eating snow or ice will lower your body temperature, so only do it to take the edge off, and steer well clear of any yellow stuff.

664. A mate of mine who's a Royal Marine told me that the Jetboil revolutionised feeding in the military; everyone had one in their spare ammo pouch, so the instant they stopped, even for just a few minutes, all you could hear were stoves firing up. By getting a 'wet' down their throats (a cup of tea to you and me), they improved hydration, got some calories in (milk and sugar) and, most importantly, it boosted morale. The same approach should be taken on alpine routes, so when you have the time and the gas, brew up! To do this, make sure you have all your brew kit in the top of your rucksack (stove, lighters, gas, tea etc.).

665. If you have a hanging stove, you can brew up anywhere, even at a hanging belay. Just pull out the stove, stuff it full of snow, and you're away.

666. With the Jetboil stove or MSR Reactor, you can drink from the pan while on the move (avoid burning your lips by adding a small patch of tape to the rim of the pan).

667. Take extra food to eat before you begin climbing as you will probably expend extra calories on the approach. The classic meal would be quick-cook pasta or noodles, along with cheese and sauce.

668. If you're sprinting up a route, think about taking an additional gas canister so you can melt extra water ready for morning brews. Starting out thirsty because you didn't bring a few grams of extra gas is just poor planning.

669. Although I find it hard to drink, Dean Potter always swore by the huge benefits of wheatgrass powder over standard sports drinks, adding a scoop of it to his water bottle before speed ascents.

670. Most stoves are fast at heating water from snow, but are even faster at heating snow to cold water. So, if fuel is low, or you just need to refill your bottles, then don't waste fuel by boiling it up. But also don't drink cold water if it may contain viruses or bacteria.

671. If you find that you often have quite a lot of water left at the end of the day in your 1-litre bottle, carry a smaller 500-millilitre Nalgene bottle instead, and, if you run out of water, just stop and refill using your stove.

672. I tend to work on two teabags a day, as teabags are light, and running out or rationing them is not good for morale. I use one for breakfast and another before eating (to get everyone hydrated), and then reuse the same one a second time before going to sleep.

673. If you think you're going to run short on teabags, just put one teabag into the pan, rather than one teabag into each person's mug.

674. If you run out of tea, melt a sweet in the boiling water to give it some taste (I know some climbers whose 'sweet tea' was all they had to eat as well!).

675. Store your milk powder in double Ziploc bags, and then store this in a third, small roll-top stuff sack. This way you won't see all your valuable milk wasted as it explodes in your bag.

676. Have a system for dishing out milk, and consider having a small spoon that lives in the milk stuff sack. Stick to one spoon per cup, and leave it up to the drinker to stir.

677. Each person should have their own spoon, and it is their responsibility to know where their spoon is. Even so, always carry a lightweight (plastic) spare.

678. Have a place where you always keep your spoon when you're not eating. For me, this is the chest pocket of my belay jacket (along with my toothbrush).

679. Having a tiny karabiner on your spoon means you can clip it off to something instead of putting it down for a moment, as a spoon 'put down' is very often not found again. If your spoon has no hole, drill one.

680. Energy gels are great for topping up your tank, but they have a nasty habit of exploding before you get to the mountain, or once you get home and they're forgotten, so get into the habit of carrying them in a plastic food box.

681. If you're undertaking a climb of over three days, switch out the meal of my Alpine FSR to a meal with more calories, ideally a dehydrated meal that can be cooked in its own pouch. These meals, although marginally heavier and expensive than carrying a load of pasta, are very light, compact, tasty and require the minimum of time to prepare. If you find yourself in a shitstorm on a ledge or stuck in a buckling tent, cooking up pasta is far from easy. With a good-quality meal (Fuizion, Mountain House, DryTech) you just pour in boiling water to the mark (around 300 millilitres), close the lid, and wait for 10 minutes. You can eat straight out of the pouch.

682. Before you pour water into the pouch, break up and mix the contents by squeezing the bag. Once water has been added, do this again.

Five-star bivvy on the Russian route, Eiger.

683. Using a long-handled spoon makes getting the food out of the bottom corners much easier.

684. Once the water is added, stick the pouch under your jacket, but don't forget to keep it upright, as having stew spill all over yourself is both wasteful and messy.

685. Once you've finished eating, fold the meal pouches and insert all of them into a single-use meal pouch, press out the air and seal.

686. You can also use meal pouches to piss in, or drink out of (though not in that order), or even fill them with snow and use them as tent anchors.

687. Chocolate is dense and heavy, and is often not a great thing to carry on a route. I tend to take along biscuits for a post-meal treat, or pre-meal 'pick me up' if the team is dog-tired. Robust biscuits like ginger biscuits are ideal – just make sure you share them out!

688. I spent five days on the Eiger attempting the Russian route in the winter of 2013 as a team of three. We had two titanium cups and one large measuring jug and at the end of the day we would elect the 'man of the day', and they would have the jug for tea and breakfast. I know that although it was bigger, the jug only held the same amount of tea as the smaller cups, but it always seemed to raise morale. What's this got to do with food? Nothing, but never lose sight of the positive psychological role that food and drink plays in a team, instead of focusing only on the raw maths of the calories.

689. When building a menu, try and have food that can be eaten in many different ways, wet and dry, hot and cold, and adapt meals and mealtime to the route.

690. Doug Scott once told me that having an evening brew and a snack worked super well in the greater ranges, meaning a team could push on into the night without the risk of hitting the wall.

FIRST AID (691–708)

691. Always carry a basic first-aid kit on a multi-day route. This should be in a small waterproof stuff sack that is marked as the first-aid kit. Inside, carry a small pair of folding scissors, six safety pins (two size 1s, three size 2s, one size 3), a small selection of plasters, one roll of Micropore tape (1.25-centimetre by 5-metre), 1 metre of duct tape wrapped around a stubby pencil or credit card, one wound dressing, mild painkillers (paracetamol/ibuprofen), a small set of tweezers (for both thorns and ticks). This should deal with minor injuries and would be used together with clothing for more serious injuries (broken bones etc.).

692. If you have a long walk, especially if you're going to be tired and dirty, say a walk out, then it may be well worth taking along a small sachet of glide cream, or a tiny tin of Vaseline, as this will stop rubbing and chafing. On one occasion, I got this so bad while walking back from Fitz Roy that I had to use our last bit of butter!

693. It's the little things that often cause the most pain on a trip, so don't take along a trauma kit and neglect to include a tiny tube of athlete's foot cream.

694. Look after your feet on a trip and they'll look after you. Try and clean them every day if you can, either by simply rubbing them with snow or with a wet wipe. Once they are dry, you should apply some talc (antifungal if you can) and then put on dry socks, and dry the wet ones in your clothing. Make sure your nails are cut short, and try to remove any thick dead skin or calluses from your feet before a trip.

695. Don't be blasé about infections when away from home, as other countries have bugs that your body may not be used to. Clean any cuts with soap and cover with Micropore tape, removing it at night to let the wound dry out if it has become wet.

696. I often use tea tree oil on my hands and feet when climbing in Yosemite, as I find this seems to deal with minor infections and athlete's foot.

697. Try and avoid sleeping in layers with low breathability, such as membrane softshells or breathable hard shells, as you'll never fully dry out and you may end up with crotch rot (or 'expedition beaver'), which will take a long time to get rid of (it's basically a fungal infection.)

698. For mountaineers, the three most important rock-solid first-aid skills are: 1) Cardiopulmonary resuscitation (CPR). 2) Identifying and dealing with early-stage hypothermia. 3) Managing suspected head and spinal injuries. Even though none of these require any specialist kit, they could save the lives of your friends – or your own life. Don't just read up on this, but go on a course and get it locked in your head.

699. Go on a first-aid course, anything from a Red Cross training day, right up to a wilderness first aid day where you learn how to sew your mates up with dental floss.

700. For multi-week trips, carry a more extensive first-aid kit that stays at the base. Include some powerful painkillers, general antibiotics, and a mini dental kit.

701. Don't go on any trip abroad without a copy of *Pocket First Aid and Wilderness Medicine* by Jim Duff and Peter Gormly – it's a real lifesaver, and I know of one team who had to carry out a medical procedure on one member's haemorrhoids using only this as a guide!

702. An 'Israeli bandage' is a good piece of gear to have in a more extensive personal first-aid kit, and definitely in an expedition kit. This bandage is a sort of 'bandage on steroids' – based on half a century of fighting and bloodshed, it is highly absorbent and can be used in many ways that an ordinary bandage can't.

703. Another modern military medical item worth looking at is QuikClot, a powder that is sprinkled on to a wound to quickly stop the bleeding. Although designed for the military, you can buy small sachets called QuikClot Sport.

704. If you need to make a makeshift splint then you can use the frame sheet inside your rucksack, tent poles, sleeping mat, or a combination of these.

705. Never underestimate the effect of shock on a casualty, as people can die in the mountains from what appear to be non-life-threatening injuries. Shock is caused by a disruption to the normal flow of blood, and can be due to many things, either severe, such as external or internal bleeding, or minor, like being involved in a traumatic incident. Signs to look for are: restlessness, nervousness, thirst, confusion, fast breathing, blue skin, nausea, vomiting, paleness, weak pulse, and sweaty but cold skin. If someone is in shock, lay them down, keep them as warm as possible and reassure them until help arrives. Don't give them anything to eat or drink, unless you've been instructed to do so.

706. In sub-zero temperatures, get into the habit of checking each other's faces to see that everything is covered, as well as monitoring people's morale and responsiveness. In very cold conditions, all skin must be covered, and food and drink needs to be taken on board every hour.

707. Take frostbite seriously once the temperature drops below -5 °C – it can come on very quickly, and once you've been nipped, then it's downhill from there. If anyone gets frostbitten, warm the area (heat pads work well), keep the area clean and free from constriction (wear socks on your hands if gloves are too tight) and seek immediate help.

708. With frostbite (modern gear means that the nose, cheeks and fingers are the main danger areas) don't be a martyr or a hero. The moment you know it's frostbitten (the skin goes waxy and numb), get in touch with mountain rescue. A 10-minute helicopter ride may mean a complete recovery in a few weeks, while a two-day descent may see you lose a lump of flesh.

STOVES, PANS AND KITCHEN STUFF (709–747)

709. Gas stoves such as the MSR XGK series work best in sub-zero temperatures as their fuel and pressure aren't affected by the cold, whereas canister stoves work better at high altitude, due to the lower air pressure and often warmer temperatures (it gets quite warm at high altitude in the daytime).

710. If you're using a canister stove below freezing, try and rotate between two canisters, one inside a jacket and one on the stove, the idea being to keep the gas as warm as possible.

711. Once you get ice build-up on the outside of your gas canister, it's time to warm it up, otherwise performance will continue to fall, and you'll end up with a rolling 'non boil'.

712. Water boils at relatively low temperatures at high altitude, so if food needs cooking well, use a pressure cooker (a vital item for base camp).

713. If your gas canister is freezing, warm it up with your hands or place it in a pan lid full of warm water (replace often), or use a heat pad held on the bottom.

714. Don't think that wrapping the canister with foam will keep the heat in, as the cold is coming from inside the canister as the gas is expelled, so covering it will only make it worse.

715. If you have to use a canister stove in sub-zero temperatures, consider making a heat exchanger by running a thin copper strip (cheap from DIY stores) through the edge of the flame and down to the canister. Only use it in very cold temperatures as putting hot metal against a thin-walled object full of high-pressure flammable gas is obviously dangerous.

716. Always have three ways of lighting your stove: a) lighter, b) matches (in a canister), c) flint and steel. You may also have a piezo igniter built into your stove, but don't expect this to last. Your main form of spark is flint and steel, which will work wet or dry, at high or low altitudes, and cannot be broken – something that can't be said for matches or lighters. Attach the flint and steel to your stove so they can't be lost.

717. Always use good-quality gas – Coleman Fuel (white gas) or MSR IsoPro isobutane, for example – and avoid filling your stove at the pump (diesel or petrol), as non-dedicated fuels always have a ton of crap in them that will mess up your stove.

718. If you have to use poor-quality fuel, always filter it first through a fuel filter funnel before putting it into your fuel bottle. Little bits of rust from old fuel containers can easily block up your stove.

719. Make sure you have a spare kit, and ideally a spare pump, if your life depends on your stove or you're using poor fuel.

720. If you're using a stove on snow then take a stove board made out of plywood. You can improve your stove's stability by adding bungee loops to hold the fuel bottle in place.

721. Carry your stove in a dedicated stuff sack, as most stoves will get very dirty and liquid stoves can leak small amounts of unburnt fuel. I have a pocket sewn into my stove sack that holds a flint and steel and a repair kit.

722. Don't trust plastic fuel containers unless they are super-heavy-duty, especially if it's below freezing.

723. Don't trust lids on fuel bottles unless they are of the MSR design.

724. Never store fuel with food, and if you're doing a carry-in, try and keep them apart.

725. Don't fill a fuel bottle inside a tent. If you must, make sure you blast some ventilation through the tent before you light up the stove, and keep the spare fuel apart from the stove.

726. Big pans work best for melting snow. Begin with a small amount of snow and gradually add more as it melts, rather than just filling it up to the top at the start.

727. Never cook food inside the same pan as the snow, as even the smallest amount of food residue can burn and taint the water you're making – and burnt water smells and tastes horrible.

728. A large aluminium kettle is great for melting snow if you're using freeze-dried food or flasks, making it easy to fill them up without spilling water.

729. Before a big trip, practise stripping down your stove and pump, so that you know how to do it when you really need to.

730. Take along a big, lightweight stuff sack or heavy-duty plastic bag (an Ikea one is ideal) to gather and hold snow to use inside your tent. This is a good idea for many reasons, the best being that the snow around the porch soon gets contaminated with fuel, toe nails and old food, and soon runs out.

731. Modern pans that feature built-in heat exchangers can produce higher levels of carbon monoxide (odourless toxic gas), so you should increase venting.

732. The main way to decrease carbon monoxide is to create enough space for the gas to combust beneath the pan. A long time ago, stoves often came with 'winter legs' – longer pan supports that meant the stove was safe to use inside a tent in winter. These days people are more focused on boil time – which is how manufacturers sell stoves to punters – rather than 'stove will not kill you!' If you're going on a big winter trip then consider making a custom housing for your stove, like a large Trangia, and lift up your pan by 2 centimetres. This support will also reduce the chance of spills.

733. If you're on a tough alpine route where you may be spread out, then take one mini hanging stove each (like a Jetboil) and use it both as your cup and stove. This system increases the speed at which you can cook and adds redundancy to your team.

734. Test all gas canisters before you commit to a route – screw them on and check they connect properly. Canisters can get damaged in transit, and realising a canister doesn't work mid-route can end a climb.

735. If you drop your pan, then the only replacement is an empty gas canister. Just cut off the valve area, and hope you didn't just bring small, 100-gram canisters!

736. If a canister isn't working then try screwing on the jet as tight as possible, as the nipple may have been pushed down while the canister was being stored in the shop or when it was shipped.

737. If you have multiple MSR stoves, double-check the burner fits the pump, as an MSR WhisperLite pump does not fit on to an XG stove (or didn't the last time I made such a mistake).

738. If your life depends on your stove, and getting hydrated, say you're on a polar trip, then take one stove per person in a team of three, or three stoves for a team of four. You can run all the stoves at the same time to decrease the time needed to cook, fill water bottles and flasks by 30 per cent, while having total redundancy in case one or even two stoves break. If you operate all your stoves simultaneously, make sure you increase venting (it'll be very hot in there, so you'll need it).

739. If it's extremely cold (-30 °C), you may have to cook inside the inner tent, placing your stove board in the centre. This will warm up the inside and make it more comfortable to move around and cook, and it will also dry gear, but remember to keep some vents open to the outside and have a strategy for an unruly stove (fire blanket etc.). Make sure the tent door is set up so you can quickly open it.

740. If you're using a Jetboil-style stove and you know it's going to get bashed around, then don't put the gas can inside the stove, because if the pan gets deformed, you'll end up with the gas jammed inside.

741. Unless you're car camping, use a stove you understand and trust, and care for it like a marine cares for his rifle.

742. When I'm doing a route using tents or flysheets (for portaledges in winter, and tent-based expeditions), I have a rule of never ever lighting the stove in the morning. Instead, each person carries a one-litre flask (thermos) and at night this is filled up (along with everyone's water bottle). In the morning you use this to make brews and there is also enough to add to porridge or cereal as well. If you have some left, you can use this to drink in the day or begin melting snow at night.

743. Only buy the best-quality flask (the biggest you can), which has top ratings for warmth – many flasks are crap and the contents just get cold.

744. The slick metal lids on flasks can be impossible to take off wearing gloves, so glue skateboard grip tape to them (or duct tape with matchsticks stuck inside to form ridges).

745. The same applies to the plastic stopper inside – models with an elliptical shape can be easier to undo.

746. If you're doing a heavy-duty trip where your flask might get banged, then wrap it in foam, as any dent will stop it from working.

747. On super-cold trips, even a well-insulated Nalgene will freeze, so a flask will be necessary.

Pulling heavy loads in Queen Maud Land, Antarctica.

SNOW TRAVEL (748-764)

748. If you're heading into an area with a lot of snow and long approaches, then avoid doing so on foot. Get some lightweight snowshoes, skis or, better still, head down to Hertz and see if you can hire a skidoo or piste basher!

749. You don't have to be able to ski in order to ski – by which I mean shuffle around on skis on the flat and on easy hills. Unless the terrain is tricky (trees and rocky ground), skiing is far easier than using snowshoes. Make sure the skis have skins, and bindings that fit your mountain boots.

750. Ski mountaineering bindings are designed to work only with ski boots and ski mountaineering boots. The issue is that only these boots will release safely in a fall, meaning if you're wearing your La Sportiva climbing boots and tackle a black run (you need to try skiing in soft boots to realise how hard that would be – even if we switch out that black run for a baby slope), if you fall you will probably rip your knees off. This is why if you ask a Chamonix ski tech about bindings for mountain boots, they will say 'non!' In reality, some bindings will fit on mountain boots which have pronounced heel and toe welts, but they will not be good enough and safe to ski downhill on, and should only be used for flat stuff and uphill skiing.

751. Instead of using a super-expensive and pretty heavy ski mountaineering kit for expeditions, use a lightweight Nordic kit and Arctic bindings designed for wearing with big non-technical boots. The classic one is the Fischer E99 ski and something like a Weber, Icetrek, Berwin or Norwegian army binding, which are bindings that simply buckle on to any boot (even approach shoes). Superglue and screw on your skins (make a small metal plate to wrap over the front edge to stop it wearing). This system is way lighter than a ski mountaineering system and has the bonus that unless you're a pro, you won't be able to ski downhill on it.

752. When it comes to the tricky area of coming downhill on your skis, probably wearing a big pack, then leave your skins on and consider increasing braking power by wrapping cord around the skis as well, making them big snow shoes. Zigzag down and take your time.

753. If you're travelling on snow, then carrying a heavy pack is stupid. Get a plastic pulk and pull that along behind you as much as you can – this will save you a great deal of energy and also enables you to take more food and kit.

754. Going downhill with a pulk can be a nightmare, as it will slide past you or into your legs at every opportunity. To avoid this, wrap cord around the pulk to act as a brake.

755. If you want a simple method of taking a pulk on an expedition without taking the bulk of a pulk, then get a sheet of high-density polyethylene and make a rollable pulk. Just cut the sheet so that it will roll around your bag or rucksack (drill holes around the edges to thread), make a tapered front edge, and roll this over the front.

756. To make a pulk harness, just clip two karabiners from the bottom of your shoulder straps or the hip tension straps, clip a 1-metre length of 5-millimetre cord to each krab, tie a figure-of-eight knot in the middle of the cord, and clip a third krab to this. Ideally, this third krab should be far enough away that you can pull it around the side of your body to clip the haul line (5- or 6-millimetre cord) from yourself to the pulk.

757. If you find yourself having to move through deep snow without skis or snowshoes, then take it easy and slow. Ideally, you need a big team to rotate at a set time based on snow depth, as anyone in front will get tired and reduce team speed. In knee-deep snow, rotating every 30 minutes is good, while in hip-deep snow, you may want to halve that.

758. If breaking trail, have the front person carry a lighter pack, or no pack at all if it's nightmare conditions. (Their pack can be ferried backwards and forwards, as you'll be going very slowly anyway.)

759. When breaking trail, make it a good trail, meaning solid steps that can be stepped into without having to post hole alone (that means breaking down the walls between the step), and keeping them tight.

760. If things get really desperate, especially in deep snow, then getting on your hands and knees will be easier – with the term 'easier' being relative.

761. In some situations it may be better to drag heavy packs behind you, as their extra weight could be making things worse, especially with near-body-weight expedition loads.

762. Deep snow travel, without skis or snowshoes, is an exercise devised by the devil himself, requiring incredible mental and physical stamina, and so the fitter and stronger you are, the better.

763. Consult maps for areas of water and be wary of any rivers unless you know they will be frozen solid; even in the coldest conditions, where you have moving water, you will have thin ice.

764. Learn to read the snow and work out which areas will be soft, which will be hard, where the breakable crust may take your weight, where you'll be up to your neck in it. Look at the lie of the land and decide which way will give you the best chance of getting to where you want to be without blowing your brains out.

EXPEDITION AND MOUNTAIN TENTS (765–802)

765. If you're camping on snow, you should dig a pit in your porch/vestibule. This will allow you to step down into the tent rather than crawl in.

766. The snow pit also creates a heat sink, with cold air flowing down into the hole, making the tent warmer.

767. You should cook with your feet in the hole, which is far more comfortable than cooking cross-legged.

768. If your stove bursts into flames, you can throw the burning stove down into your tent pit, saving your tent flysheet. If you have your shovel close by, you can throw some snow on to it if it keeps misbehaving.

769. Tents are pretty hard to set on fire, but even so, don't try to find out for yourself as they are quite easily damaged. When priming stoves or using gas stoves, give the operation the utmost attention – having a second pair of hands to ignite the stove is a good idea.

770. Always have a pan or a pan lid handy to chuck on the flame if it gets out of control, or even carry a small section of fire blanket (you can buy small fire blankets for yachting).

771. If you're facing some major storms, consider double-poling your tent. For extended expedition camping, a tunnel tent is best, as all poles are the same length. If double-poled, even if two poles break you will still have three left, plus a spare.

772. Always carry two spare pole sections for broken poles, as well as both metal and plastic zip ties for improvised repairs. You can improvise pole repairs with a cut-up gas canister. Cut the top and bottom off the canister and then break open the cylinder and finally roll up the cylinder to make a tight tube. Secure with zip ties (metal zip ties work best) or gaffer tape.

773. If you're using pulks, gaffer tape your tent poles together so they break apart in the middle and the length matches that of the pulk. With the tent rolled up, leave them threaded through the tent and, at the end of the day, you can pop these single sections together and you're away.

774. On a super-cold trip, it's easy for tent poles to freeze together, doubly so if you're using a single-skinned tent with internal poles. To unfreeze, just rub your hand up and down the pole for a few seconds until the bond melts.

775. The bungee cord in tent poles can grow slack, meaning it won't connect properly, which can lead to breakages. By pulling the bungee backwards and forwards for a few seconds, you should get enough friction to return some elasticity.

776. To avoid poles not fitting together all the way (the number-one reason for poles breaking – apart from drunk people falling on your tent), put a strip of bright tape on either side of the join or even a little spray of paint. This way, if you see the halves of the tape/paint don't meet, you know the poles aren't joined.

777. If you're using your tent in exposed places, for example on mountain ledges, the poles can be very easily dropped, and without them most tents don't work that well. For this reason, tape a clip-in loop to both ends of each pole so they can be secured once you get them out.

778. Don't rely on the little zip pullers on most tents, as these are meant for summer camping. Instead, add full-on 3-millimetre zip pullers so you can get into your tent even when wearing big mitts.

779. Three-millimetre tent underlay foam is super light and dramatically increases both tent warmth and comfort. It is perfect for base camp or polar use. If someone loses a mat, or their foam mat goes flat, you should be able to fold this up to form a full-depth mat (an expedition mat is around 12 millimetres thick, so the foam will need folding four times).

780. Just because a tent is advertised as being a four-season tent, don't expect it to last a winter storm. This will depend primarily on the strength of the seams used in the fly and how well the guys are sewn in (as well as how many guys the tent has). You also need to pitch it with its smallest profile to the wind, and fully guy it, and even then it may not survive unless you dig a snow wall.

781. If you use skis to secure the guy lines to your tent, always have the binding facing away from the tent, otherwise the sharp edges on the skis will cut into your guy lines.

782. You can buy fancy winter pegs for tents (that can be placed normally, but generally work better placed sideways as deadmen), but medium-thickness bamboo works just as well. Mark all bamboo with reflective tape to act as a guide if you're trying to find your tent at night.

783. Mini Clamcleats are perfect for guy lines as they pull tight easily and lock down hard. If your tent doesn't feature them, then buy some and add them yourself.

784. Super-thin guys tangle easily and can cause many problems – more than one person has got frostbite trying to untangle guys. First off, never tie them up when packing the tent; either leave them loose or make some little stuff sacks (like you get on Exped tents) that you can stuff the guys into (these little netting bags should be attached to the guys so they can't be lost).

785. Replace the super-skinny, 1-millimetre guy line cord with thicker, reflective 4-millimetre reflective guys made by Clamcleat, as they are less prone to tangles, far more robust and much stronger.

786. For long-term use, having a tarp placed just above the porch or close to the tent can create more dry space.

787. A good system for setting up a tarp in an A-frame setup is to have a length of 4-millimetre cord running through the middle of the tarp (threaded through the centre tie-offs) and secured with a prusik loop (formed from 2-millimetre cord) at each end. This will form the central span of the tent. Secure the 4-millimetre cord to two objects, then simply pull the two prusik loops tight to tension the tent. Now just attach cord or 4-millimetre bungee to the corners to secure the tarp.

788. If you carry extra bamboo, you can use this to support your tarp either in single sections or taped together (you can run the tarp over the porch and hold two edges up with bamboo).

789. When living in a tent for long periods, it's vital that people respect each other's space – ideally, each person should have their own tent. If forced in together, make good use of stuff sacks, with each person keeping their vital day-to-day kit at the head of their sleeping bags.

790. You can construct pretty good tent shelving using yachting netting (pulpit netting), securing it in the roof of the tent. This is the warmest part of a tent and is both a good place to dry stuff or to simply stop stuff from freezing. Just don't overload it.

791. Snow valances make it a little easier to pile snow or rocks around the tent, but they reduce ventilation and add weight and cost. I've used tents with and without valances in terrible conditions and feel that they aren't really necessary as long as you pile snow up around the edge of the tent carefully.

792. If you have to dig your tent out in a storm, take great care not to go anywhere near the fly with your shovel. In cold weather, your flysheet will be more fragile and it can be easily damaged. Keep the shovel blade away from the tent, and use a gloved hand to clear the snow nearest the fly.

793. If your flysheet is ripped, you will need your repair kit close at hand, so make sure you know where it is. Duct tape will not work in a storm, as snow will stick to the glue, which may not be sticky anyway due to the cold. To make a fast repair, you will need to loosen the fly so it has some give, then try to clip it together, pulling and rolling the two sides and then holding them. You can try securing them with a number of items that may be worth carrying, including plastic freezer bag clips, plastic bottle tops (cut off the top section of Coke bottles) or old-school large safety pins. Once secure, it may be worth shovelling snow over that section of the tent to protect it.

794. Once the weather is better, you can try to repair a damaged flysheet. In order to do this, make sure you have some spare nylon in your repair kit (either a large piece of nylon or a roll of spinnaker fabric), which you can sew over the hole. First get the fabric nice and dry, stick both sides together with duct tape and then sew a strip of fabric over the lot (so that the needle passes through the fly, the repair fabric and the duct tape). It will be a messy repair, but it should hold.

795. If you have Seam Grip (Shoe Glu, Seam Seal, Aquaseal etc.) then also carry some mosquito netting in your repair kit. To repair a fly, stick gaffer tape on the outside of the damaged area, coat the inside with Seam Grip, stick the netting over the Seam Grip and add some more. Once set, the repair will be stronger than the tent!

796. Keep a small brush handy in your tent for clearing out dirt, snow and ice. This can also be used before you get into the tent to clear ice and snow from your clothing. On an alpine route, a little brush is still worth carrying in winter as it can be used to brush snow off the rock as well. Make sure it has a sharp, narrow tip at the handle end so you can use it to scrape hard ice off boots and zippers before you get into the tent.

797. A small sponge is handy if you get a lot of condensation (for example, when cooking) and will come in super handy when someone inevitably spills their tea.

798. Keep the bottom of your tent in a good shape when camping on hard ground by using a groundsheet to protect your tent floor. It's not really worth buying one; instead make one from a cut-open large survival bag. Make sure the footprint of the groundsheet is smaller than that of the tent floor, otherwise moisture will collect at the edges and migrate under the tent.

799. If your tent stuff sack is too small, get a larger stuff sack, as trying to fit a wet tent into a small bag is a pain in the arse and will make you not want to take the tent out again to dry it.

800. No matter how dry you think your tent was when you put it away, it's always worth letting it hang for 24 hours in your house when you get home. Moisture can linger in strange places and will cause your nice tent to get smelly.

801. If you're using a bivvy tent on a very small ledge, you don't have to use it conventionally, lying side by side. It may work better if everyone sits with their back against the mountain and their feet outstretched, rather than just having an open bivvy.

802. The Russians employ an ice hammock on steep routes where snow ledges can't be dug deep enough for a tent (or where such ledges would take all day to dig). The design is just like a hammock, and snow, ice and even rocks are piled into it as the ledge is chopped out, extending the ledge by a few feet – which can make a big difference!

Portaledge bivvy, day 10 on Holstind, Antarctica.

Ingeborg Jakobsen cleaning a pitch on Holstind, Antarctica.

Sinead Rickerby on *Lucky Streaks*, Fairview Dome, Tuolumne Meadows.

007

TRAINING (803–876)

"Record all your training sessions — total weight lifted, kilometres covered, calories burnt — everything that gives a good indication of the quality of the session."

TRAINING (803-876)

OVERCOMING FEAR (803-810)

803. Being scared can be a big part of climbing; after all, very often you're putting yourself in hazardous places. If you're going to climb well, you need to get a handle on how you cope with fear and anxiety, otherwise you'll never get up anything, and even if you do, you won't enjoy it! Just as you would put some time into sorting out your rack, you should also put some time and effort into sorting out your head.

804. Very often, before a hard climb or a crux pitch, you'll feel anxiety in the pit of your stomach, a feeling that makes you want to give in before you've even tried. These are very important moments in any venture, as it's here that you'll probably fail or let someone else take over. Instead of letting this feeling of deep dread and terror take over, flip the feeling and think of it as excitement – after all, isn't it exciting?

805. This feeling of dread is understandable; you should acknowledge it and appreciate that what it is telling you is to be careful – not to turn back. Think of it as part of your psychological warm up – your primitive brain is spinning up and, once you start, it will settle down. Think of it as 'brain pump'.

806. Very often, it's good to have a supportive voice in your head, even a bullying one – a voice that drowns out the negative voices that can colour your actions. I use this mainly while training, but it can come in handy when climbing, especially when you're at your weakest mentally. To do this, create a fully functional, motivational character that is stored in your mind for those moments when you have no motivation to continue. This character can be someone you know, and if so, it will be someone you respect – someone tougher, harder and more able than you. It can also be a fictional person, who you wouldn't want or dare to let down, or an amalgamation of people. When I'm training, I often conjure up the vision of Gunnery Sergeant Hartman from *Full Metal Jacket* when I know I must try harder – I imagine him pacing me, pushing me, or just plain beating me up in order to get the most out of a session. I use this 'virtual' drill sergeant to push and praise me when I know I've gone beyond what I was capable of alone. On a route, I often imagine Cassin or Desmaison telling me to just 'get on with it', as if they know it's fine.

807. I know it sounds cheesy, but a lot of pro athletes I know use Eminem's *Lose Yourself* track to psyche themselves up before a big race. I used to think this was funny and a bit naff, until one day on the Troll Wall I found myself one hook move away from easy ground, but convinced that the hook (a tiny edge about the size of a match head) would rip. I hung there for several minutes, not daring to get on the hook, knowing that time was running out (I'd been on the route for ten days and really wanted it to end). And right then, that song's opening lyrics came into my head. And that was it, I just thought, 'no, I'm not going to let one move stop me,' and I moved on to the hook. The hook held, and we climbed the route.

808. You can fail long before you ever get to the crux or the route itself – the very idea of doing the climb can be enough to stop you dead. Don't let what you think you know about a route get in the way of finding out the truth. No route is as long, as steep, or as blank as that route you hold in your mind. Remember that even the greatest climbers put their trousers on one leg at a time.

809. When I set my sights on a big climbing project, I do so months, even years, before I know I'll get there, and it would be very easy to backtrack in the time in-between the idea and the action. How do I stay on course? Well, I visualise a gnarled old hand on the rudder of a fishing boat, the hand belonging to some salty sea dog who is scared of nothing, who heads out to sea no matter what, a man as hard and emotional as stone. When my psyche begins to flounder, I imagine this hand – just the hand – unmoving on that wooden rudder. I see the spray, the sea crashing down, the wind howling, and yet the hand remains clamped down hard and unmoving. This fisherman's course is set and immovable; he has complete trust in his skills and utter confidence in his course. This fisherman is the navigator of your dream, and whenever you begin to doubt, think of him, and keep on. (*Figure 26*)

810. Don't view a hard climb as a whole, but instead break it down into its parts: its pitches, its moves. A climb or a mountain is not alive with anything but the myths and legends of those who climbed it first, and the tales of those climbs (more often than not, heavily embellished). The climber Brutus once said, 'One route, one pitch, one move at a time,' and this is the approach you should take. Don't let the weight of a climb crush you.

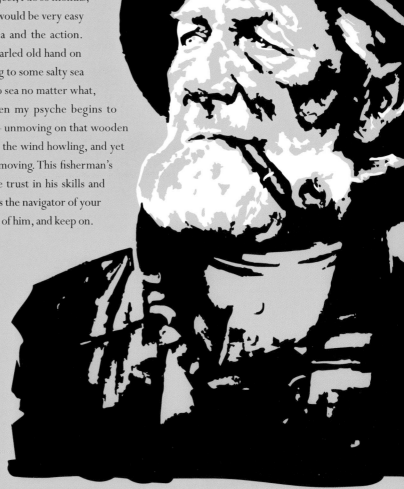

FIGURE 26

STRENGTH TRAINING (811–841)

811. If you're setting out on getting stronger outside of climbing, then the first thing to do is join a good gym, ideally a gym that's close by and cheap enough to keep up a membership.

812. When choosing a gym, don't be dazzled by fancy machines and steam rooms. What you want is a good selection of quality free weights and benches (make sure they have multiple sets, so when it's busy you don't have to wait), rowing and running machines, kettlebells and medicine balls. Having a swimming pool is nice, but gyms without a pool tend to be cheaper. Local council gyms can be very good, but if you're going to be going at least three times a week, or even every day, then having a membership is best. *(Figure 27)*

813. Strength training is the best way to prevent getting injured while climbing, as you avoid the tendency to create imbalances if only climbing, as well as strengthening all those small muscles and connectors that are rarely used on the crag or wall.

FIGURE 27

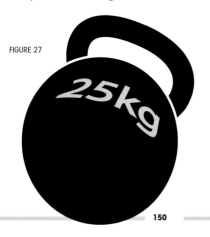

814. You need to be focused on free weights, as these will work the most muscles and improve stability and core strength, but if you want to improve your base strength, then spend a month using weight machines, as these reduce the likelihood of injury brought about by training.

815. If embarking on a new routine of strength training, then find yourself a partner, as it's much easier if you're not doing it alone. Working with a motivated partner helps to keep up the momentum and creates competition and support. If your training partner is also your climbing partner, then you'll further strengthen that bond.

816. Make your next big trip, climb or expedition the focus of your training, working out what you need to do to be more effective, then working towards that goal for one or two months.

817. If you commit to a block of training, then have some sort of forfeit if you miss training. Don't accept excuses from yourself or others, and make it clear that if someone doesn't turn up, they must have a good excuse.

818. Make the most of people in the gym, asking for their advice on training systems and correct form (vital!). This includes both staff and those people who look like they know what they're doing, especially when it comes to good form.

819. It might make you feel like a newbie, but having a few sessions with a good trainer will pay dividends, allowing you to learn faster and reducing the chance of injuries caused by inexperience.

820. At the same time, you need to realise that most people in a gym are simply training for the sake of it – to be fit. You, on the other hand, are looking to develop functional fitness – stronger legs, stronger back and hands, and better cardio so you don't get tired mid-crux. If someone tells you to do three sets of one of your max (meaning if you can deadlift 150 kilograms, you would lift 150 kilograms once, have a rest, then do that a further two times), you would get strong at lifting something heavy, but not at moving your body up a rock or an ice route. So listen to what people say, but filter it before applying it to what you're doing – and what you're trying to achieve.

821. For climbing, you're aiming to achieve good strength and conditioning: the ability to be strong and mobile over many moves, many pitches and perhaps many days. This means you don't want pure strength, but a mix of strength (a pull-up), endurance (another pull-up straight after the other), and conditioning (two pull-ups, followed by a sprint up a route at the climbing wall, followed by another two pull-ups before you have got your breath back).

822. Keep all strength sessions under an hour, with 45 minutes being the optimum. If you're training hard, anything beyond that will have limited results. Just warm up, then hit half a dozen exercises super hard and finish with some stabilising exercises. If you add warming up and warming down, no gym visit should last more than 90 minutes. It's about quality, not quantity.

823. People talk about how many sets and reps are best, but you should perhaps think more about the total weight moved per session, as on a climb you may never do a single, one-arm pull-up, but your arm may have to do 40 per cent of a one-arm pull-up several thousand times. For me, I think I need a mix of strength, endurance and power, so I tend to go for the classic three sets of five (three repetitions of an exercise done five times, with a rest in-between) or five sets of five.

824. When strength training, there is a very high chance that you will injure yourself unless you progress slowly and carefully. The big multi-muscle exercises can be very dangerous if done incorrectly or if you have some strength imbalance, so make sure your form is perfect before you attempt these, even if that means spending weeks doing the exercises with very light weights (or even just a stick).

825. One thing to focus on when undertaking the lifting of anything heavy is that you need the weight as close to your centre of gravity as possible (i.e. over your feet). Imagine a white safe area that surrounds your feet. If the weight (such as a heavy deadlift bar) is moving within this area, then you're fine. Then imagine a grey area that extends 6 inches beyond this, where any weight would not be directly over your body. Lifting or lowering anything in this area requires greater strength and more balance, calling on smaller muscles to stabilise the lifter, meaning a greater chance of injury. Beyond this is the red zone, where you should not lift anything, the area where backs are pulled, or shoulders overloaded.

826. Focus on the most important exercises, ideally the ones that hit major muscle groups at the same time (a compound exercise). Of these, the deadlift, back squat and almost anything using a kettlebell are best.

827. Never do a dumbbell curl – it does nothing at all.

828. Throw some pull-ups and press-ups in with your training, but avoid doing too many pull-ups as they're a great way to get injured. Instead, try to focus on developing overall fitness first, then tweak it.

829. If you're trying to build up your pull-up, do pull-up ladders at your max, then one less, working down to one. You can also do one every 10 or 15 seconds, which will allow you to have a higher rate per hour than just banging off sets.

830. Never drop down hard on to your arms when doing pull-ups, and always aim for good form.

831. Always warm up before any exercise by first raising your heart rate via some moderate cardio (bike, run, quick walk or row), then doing the following (sets x repetitions @ intensity): 1x5 @ 40%, 1x5 @ 50%, 1x5 @ 60%.

832. When you've finished, don't forget to warm down and stretch, as this will remove toxins from your muscles and will prevent injuries and DOMS (delayed onset muscle soreness).

833. If you want to climb every other day, don't train to failure but close to it. If you just want to train hard, try to make your last set a real killer, inching the weight up until you've completed your set.

834. Strength training is all about good form. Doing an exercise badly is a great way to injure yourself and look like a newbie.

835. If you progress too fast, you will get injured because although you can build muscle very quickly, your tendons can't keep up. For example, within a month or two of strength training, I could deadlift 100 kilograms x 100 times (20x5 @ 80%) – which was cool until I got such bad 'golfer's elbow' that I could hardly open the fridge. You should instead try working below your max for the first month (say 85%), then at your max the following month, then push it up by 5% month by month from then on. With all such training, if in doubt, play it safe and play a long game.

836. If you're working on a program, then hit the gym three or four times a week and work on a three-week system of one easy week, one moderate week and one heavy week (each week just make things harder!).

837. If you want to build solid conditioning while training with a slight reduction in strength, keep all rests to 30 seconds. But if you're more interested in building strength, then take 3-minute rests between sets. Use a stopwatch and keep to a fixed rest period.

838. Never train when ill or when getting over illness, as this is a great way to end up with chronic fatigue, plus nothing you do will be of any value.

839. A lot of male – and quite a few female – climbers are obsessed with having amazing abs and so do tons of sit-ups. Abs and general definition depend on what you eat, not your training; if you can reduce your body fat, you'll find you have abs with no training at all! If you work hard on both lowering your body fat and getting stronger, these will join up in the form of visible, rock-solid abs.

840. Never show off or compete in the gym unless you know you will easily win!

841. When weight training, avoid using gloves or tape or straps, as getting strong hands and grip strength is what you're after. If you can't hold the bar, then strengthen your hands first.

Dinnertime for Aleks Gamme on the Troll Wall.

FOOD (842–857)

842. If you need to lose weight before a big trip, either because being light would be good or for the psychological boost, set up a plan two months before. For most people who are overweight, it's easy to lose 10 per cent of their bodyweight quite quickly with the minimum of work.

843. When losing weight, it's perhaps better to focus on the idea of 'losing fat', or, better still, 'transforming' fat into muscle, as hard training will result in weight loss, but also weight gain via muscle development. If you only want to lose weight, then your training should avoid putting on too much muscle, as this tends to be counter-productive for climbers. Don't turn into a meathead bodybuilder. You need muscles that are as small and powerful as possible.

844. When I lived with an athlete, I soon realised that the more data you have, and more importantly the more data that you record, the better you can judge what works, how fast it works, and how to make it work better. So data is vital. Record your pre-breakfast weight every morning and write this down on a sheet of paper in your bathroom. Don't view this as an accurate record of how heavy, how fat or how fit you are, but simply as data. If I go from heavy eating to heavy training and mild fasting, I can lose 2 kilograms in 48 hours. *(Figure 28)*

845. Record all your training sessions – total weight lifted, kilometres covered, calories burnt – everything that gives a good indication of the quality of the session.

846. If you're aiming to slim down, then make the bulk of your training medium length (30 to 60 minutes) every day, and aim to keep your heart rate at around 45 to 65 per cent of your max. For me, that would be doing a 10-kilometre run in 1 hour or a 10-kilometre row in 40 minutes. Doing this every day will be tough at first, but you will be getting very fit without getting injured, and, as a bonus, you will be losing weight. Do this five or six days a week.

847. While training hard, try to avoid any white food, such as bread, pasta, rice and potatoes. Try to eat only food that goes off – and the quicker it goes off, the better. Hit the omega-3s, eating plenty of fish, and add seeds to meals (hemp, sesame, chia). A lot of people have tried a Paleo diet, cutting out all carbs, but this is just too extreme for most people. I'd go for the Paul Tattersall diet. Paul was the guy I first climbed El Cap with and who had the arms of a dry-stone-waller and the body of a twelve-year-old. For this diet, you just need to eat as much chicken and fish, vegetables and lentils (any colour – with my favourite being moong dal) as you can, as well as beans (black-eyed, baked, whatever). This diet is something that works for me, but might be a non-starter if you have 1 per cent body fat – in that case maybe you should only eat white food!

848. For breakfast, I drink a milkshake made from a banana, half a pint of milk, some oats, cinnamon, a spoon of honey, goji, pumpkin and flax mix – which amazingly seems to keep me going until lunchtime.

849. Get into the habit of eating all the time and eating fruit every few hours. Your aim should be to have six small meals each day. For me, this means lunch could be a cheese omelette or an apple at 11 a.m. and a tin of tuna fish at 1 p.m. Just make it as healthy as you can, but don't worry about adding some crap (curry, chocolate, cakes) as long as this isn't all you're eating.

850. For dinner, I want to eat food that I like and which fills me up but isn't going to leave me feeling bloated and tired. Again, go for as many veggies as you can, and include fish and chicken.

851. Don't starve yourself and don't cut out all the crap; like when training, your body needs to be kept off balance – so keep throwing in some good-quality crap now and again.

852. One of my favourite meals is fried chicken with some boiled broccoli, mixed together with sesame seeds and soy sauce. Sounds boring, but it's super filling and healthy, plus it tastes very nice.

853. A favourite lunch is just grated carrot, a tin of tuna, small tomatoes and some decent salad dressing. Cheap, quick, tasty and filling.

854. You can also make an Argentinean staple: just boil some eggs, add grated carrot and some dressing.

855. Don't be afraid of fat – it's not fat that got you into the state you find yourself. Instead, be aware of simple carbs and steer clear of rice, pasta and bread as much as you can.

856. When losing weight, ignore your fatness and just think of this layer of fat as unimportant to the overall plan. Focus instead on the muscle below, and work on developing that. Sure, you may look fat, but you know after a month of rowing and running that you are in fact as fit as a butcher's dog.

857. Don't confuse being fit with being healthy, or being fat with being unfit. What you're aiming for is a balance between all three.

FIGURE 28

ENDURANCE TRAINING (858–876)

858. For climbing, rowing is one of the best exercises, hitting the legs' pushing muscles, the back, the arms' pulling muscles, the heart and lungs.

859. As your fitness improves, begin adding a new set of exercises to each session until you're working your cardio endurance as well as building strength. Begin with a ladder of push-ups (important for rowing) doing 10-9-8-7-6-5-4-3-2-1 (30 seconds' rest in-between) after each session, then throw in box jumps, burpees, lunges and sit-ups. Next, add some kettlebells to your session, and lastly deadlifts, squats and bench presses, aiming for five sets of five.

860. Eventually, you should be doing a sub-hour endurance cardio followed by a 20-minute circuit every day, five or six days a week, meaning less than an hour and a half each day. You would not want to keep this up for months, but as an accelerated weight loss/strength gain program, I find it works, losing me weight (I can go from 100 kilograms to 90 kilograms in two months) and helping me feel far more healthy before a big trip.

861. The longer you spend on a climb, the more important it is to have a good endurance base, which is either built up by doing lots of that style of climbing, or by training your base. By training your endurance before a climbing trip, you will increase your chances of both pulling off the climb, as well as staying safer and more effective in a demanding environment.

862. We're told endurance increases with age, but I think this is also perhaps due to the fact that the older you are, the more self-aware you are of your body. This means that older climbers will pace themselves much better over a route, where younger climbers would not, with youthful enthusiasm making them believe they are stronger or more fit than they really are. Even if you're not that old, it's worth making a note of this and trying to slow things down, saving your energy for when it's needed.

863. A second advantage of age and experience is that you will have more experience of going into the red or hitting the wall, so when you do, you will know to expect it and how it will affect you.

864. Train your endurance the same as every army in the world does, and include a core of running into your training, building up slowly at first and constantly changing the components to keep your body off balance (once you get used to any exercise then you need to change something), meaning speed, distance and elevation. If you go out every day and do the same route at the same speed, then your body will adapt and stop growing.

865. If you're running, buy good-quality shoes and get them fitted by someone who knows about running. If you run a lot, replace them every six months.

866. Running is not all about distance, but rather quality. A stiff run for 40 minutes with your heart rate up high is better than a 2-hour slog where your heart rate is almost normal and you're just shuffling along.

867. If you want to get serious about your running, then add strength training into your program to avoid injury. Do squats, deadlifts and leg presses to develop strength and stability, and adjust it for the type of climbing you're doing, with many more repetitions (10 to 20) and less weight for endurance stuff, and fewer reps (three to five) and heavier weights for strength.

868. Running stairs is a great way to train and really sucks the life out of you. To do this, you need a long-ish flight of stairs (I use some steps in a park close to my house), ideally on your normal running route, but you can use stairs in a building (I know many people who've trained like this at work in their lunch break). Do reps on the stairs making a note of your times, aiming to go as fast as you can. You'll find that as you climb the stairs, you'll feel your tank emptying as you work your anaerobic system (high demand) which can only perform for a limited period, until you feel like you can't even walk up them anymore. Once you've done a set, slowly walk back down and take a breather then repeat. This kind of training is especially valuable for 'mountain sprints' where you have to move quickly over terrain that is dangerous and exposed. *(Figure 29)*

FIGURE 29

Photo: John Coefield

869. Set yourself goals and monitor how well you're developing as a runner, running routes or circuits that you know, and checking your times. This will allow you to judge how well you're doing.

870. Big mountain walks, especially long-distance walks such as the Welsh 14 Peaks or the Bob Graham Round, are perfect for building endurance while at the same time forming a strong team and developing navigation skills. They're also great fun and bloody knackering.

871. Use circuit training to develop both strength and endurance, mixing a bunch of exercises over an hour, with minimal rests in-between, to hit the areas that need hitting. When doing circuits, you should be moving on to the next exercise before you have had the chance to fully recover, then rest between each set – a thirty-second rest being the shortest rest you can take, and a three-minute rest allowing your heart rate to return to near normal. Work with a partner and swap exercises as you go.

872. Load carrying is a great way to stress your body and fits well into activity-specific training if you're going on an expedition or a route with a long approach. To avoid damaging your knees, focus primarily on fast uphill walking with a load, carrying water with large plastic camping carriers – then dump the water before heading back downhill. You can walk or run downhill to finish.

873. When doing load carrying, set yourself some targets. You can base these on the UK military fitness test, which is carrying 25 kilograms over 12.8 kilometres in under 1 hour and 50 minutes. If you manage that, then train up for a 2-day advanced test of 20 kilometres (30-kilogram load) in under 3 hours and 30 minutes, then on day two, 20 kilometres (20-kilogram load) in under 3 hours. If you can pull that off, then you should be fit for any expedition.

874. If you want to be as fit as a Gurkha (super-gnarly Nepalese soldiers in the British Army), then select a 5-kilometre-long uphill course with a height gain of 450 metres and do it in 48 minutes – oh and don't forget to carry 25 kilograms of rocks on your back. They also run 2.4 kilometres in under 9 minutes and 40 seconds, so get that nailed first (not sure if that's with or without their Foxtrot Oscar knife).

875. Hit the rowing machine if you're at the gym, as it is low impact but really hammers the body, heart and mind. Set yourself the target of doing 100 kilometres on the rower in 10 days, doing an easy 1 kilometre to warm up, then 10 kilometres hard (aim for a sub-40-minute time), then finish with an easy 1.5-kilometre warm down. This will give you 100 kilometres in 10 days, with two rest days.

876. Cycling is great cross training, both road biking and mountain biking. Hitting the hills is the way to go, but don't neglect other training; I find cycling is very specific and can tend to just produce very strong cyclists – plus many climbers seem to have no fear going downhill and tend to break themselves.

Vanessa Sumner on *Mega Bleam*, Lembert Dome, Tuolumne Meadows.

Kjersti Eide skinning up Devold Peak, Queen Maud Land's highest peak.

Max Biagosch happy to be up on *The Nose*, El Cap.

008

STUFF (877–1001)

*"Make it fun. Or as fun as
you can make it."*

DON'T TRY THIS AT HOME (877–879)

877. I once read a technique in a French climbing magazine about doing full-length retrievable raps using just a single rope. It went like this: tie a fifi hook to the end of your rope using a figure-of-eight knot. Now attach a piece of 5-millimetre bungee cord through the release hole in the head of the fifi (a hole used to pull a fifi off the gear it's attached to). Now tie a French prusik knot in the bungee and thread it on to the rope below the fifi hook. Attach your belay device to the rope. Hang the hook on to the anchor and weight it fully. Now pull the bungee prusik knot down the rope until it's tight. Abseil down the rope **never** taking your hand off the rope, even for an instant. On reaching the ground, take your weight off the rope. The bungee cord should now pull the fifi hook back and off the anchor and the rope will fall down to you. When I first read this I couldn't believe anyone would be stupid or brave enough to ever use it – but since then I've rapped off a tied-off knifeblade hammered in no deeper than an inch, off retrievable ice screws (a screw with the rope just looped over the hanger), and on rope with a core splling out like intestines – so who am I to judge? Needless to say, if you try this, I think you have a 90 per cent chance of dying. *(Figure 30)*

878. A 'poor man's GriGri' is a technique used to create an auto-locking belay device, and is really only of use to big-wall climbers whose partner is moving at glacial speed, or maybe for some imagined self-rescue scenario, say a partner who has to belay but who may fall unconscious at any time. To do this, you need two belay devices. Simply feed the ropes from one into the other and clip a karabiner into the rope(s) between the two. To pay out rope, pull the karabiner to get some slack through the first belay device, then pull this slack out through the second. *(Figure 31)*

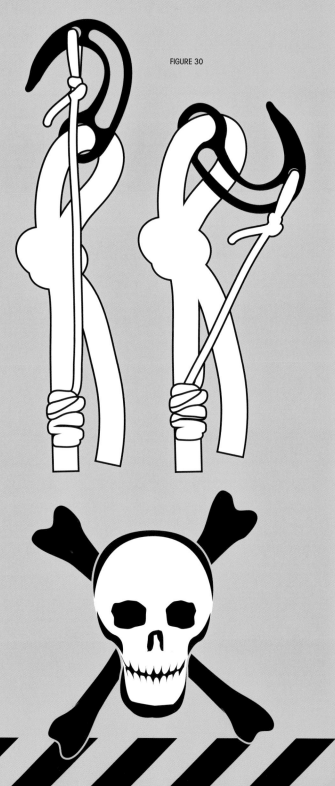

FIGURE 30

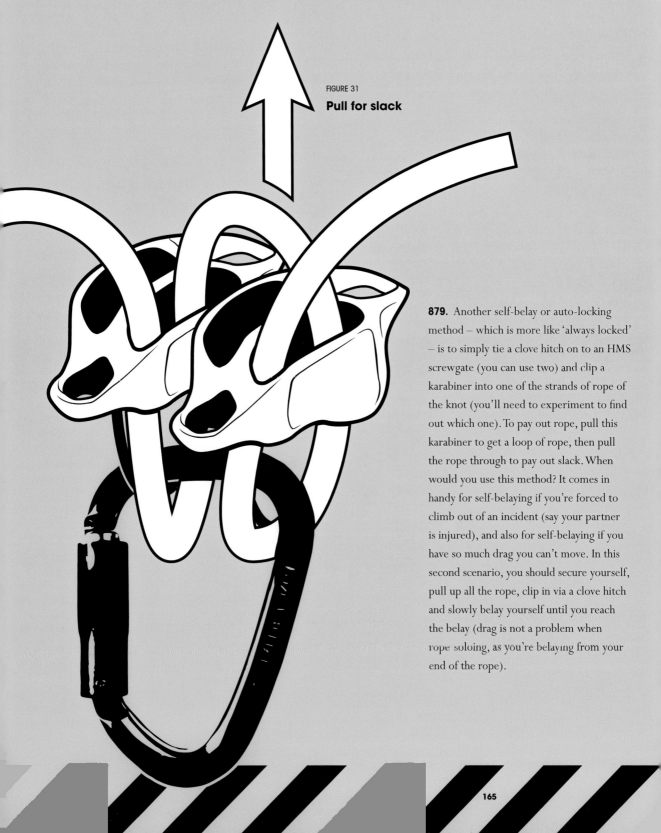

FIGURE 31

Pull for slack

879. Another self-belay or auto-locking method – which is more like 'always locked' – is to simply tie a clove hitch on to an HMS screwgate (you can use two) and clip a karabiner into one of the strands of rope of the knot (you'll need to experiment to find out which one). To pay out rope, pull this karabiner to get a loop of rope, then pull the rope through to pay out slack. When would you use this method? It comes in handy for self-belaying if you're forced to climb out of an incident (say your partner is injured), and also for self-belaying if you have so much drag you can't move. In this second scenario, you should secure yourself, pull up all the rope, clip in via a clove hitch and slowly belay yourself until you reach the belay (drag is not a problem when rope soloing, as you're belaying from your end of the rope).

GUIDING PRINCIPLES OF ANDY KIRKPATRICK (880–894)

880. *Survivability*. Basically make yourself, your team and your kit as survivable as possible. This goes against many alpine-style principles (fast and light) and probably comes from me learning my trade as a winter alpine climber. This means having clothing and sleeping bags that will work when wet (so no down), a stove that will not break and can be used in terrible conditions (MSR XG or MSR Reactor stove – in fact any MSR stove), knowing how to stay alive in any situation, and having the skills to either get down and/or deal with problems. The more difficult you are to kill, the longer you will live.

881. *Redundancy*. Have a backup plan for everything and work out beforehand what you would do if X happens. Don't put all your eggs in one basket.

882. *Paranoia*. Plan for the worst and expect bad things to happen, and you'll be surprised how much easier reality is. I always carry a full winter kit when climbing El Cap (full shell, fleece, belay jacket, fleece bottoms etc.). I've only had to use it once, but on that occasion (trying to climb *Tangerine Trip* in a day – which became three days), we got stuck in a major winter storm; without the winter kit we would have died. And I know this because we almost got hypothermia even while wearing all the kit. Being an optimist is vital when it comes to tackling big climbs, but plan as a pessimist.

883. *Having no plan is a plan*. The key to success and survival is adaptation: the ability to change your plan to suit a changing route, changing weather, or the mood of partners and reality. Have all the pieces you need to win, but keep your strategy loose and flexible because things will change.

884. *Do what it takes*. If you want to succeed, it will usually take a superhuman effort to make it happen, meaning going beyond what you think you can do – going longer, harder and higher. If you don't think you can do this, or your partners can't keep up, then don't try.

885. *Never be afraid to back down*. But before you do, count to ten and double-check you're backing down for the right reasons and not just because you're being tested and you think you're failing.

886. *Leave climbing behind now and again*. Try something new, like kayaking, mountain biking or swinging. Sometimes it's good to be a novice, to remember how to learn new things.

887. *Make it fun*. Or as fun as you can make it.

888. *If you're the leader then look after your team and set a high standard*. Do the crap you'd like them to do, but do it better and do it first.

889. *Toast failure, because success brings its own rewards*. Failing goes hand in hand with doing anything worthwhile, and it can be almost as rewarding. So when you get down safe, acknowledge what you've tried to do and learn from it.

890. *Seize opportunities*. Kurt Vonnegut once said 'peculiar travel suggestions are dancing lessons from God'. Embrace any opportunity that comes your way or which you can manufacture, and try not to let work, money or time get in the way of gold medal moments all the time.

891. *Never be dogmatic.* Always be open to new ideas and new tricks.

892. *Be creative in everything you do.* From building a belay, to climbing a pitch, to picking objectives.

893. *Smile.* If you haven't laughed or smiled for 24 hours, you need to rethink what you're doing.

894. *Don't crack up.* When doing dangerous routes, remember that the first sign of a nervous breakdown is waking up screaming, only to realise you're not asleep!

CHOOSING A GUIDE OR CLIMBING COURSE (895–901)

895. Before you go down the route of employing an individual or an organisation, or signing up for a commercial trip, ask yourself what you really want out of it. If it's training, then a mountaineering instructor may be best, as they can tailor a day or several days that could fill in the gaps in your knowledge. If it's experience and training you're after, then getting a guide for a few days and telling them the things you'd like to climb and learn so you can do it yourself may be better. For example, going out to an ice climbing area for a week with a good guide means you can second routes way harder than you could lead and at the same time you can see how they do it, and perhaps lead some easy ice under their tutorship. Most UK alpine guides I know actively want their clients to learn from them. If it's more experience and less knowledge that you're after, getting a guide to do as much mileage as possible, or going on a group trip somewhere on a commercial expedition, may suit you better, as generally the more people in a group, the less time the leader or guide will have to answer questions.

Tormod Granheim having trouble with his bowels on the Troll Wall.

896. When booking a trip or employing a guide, make sure you don't bullshit them – it will soon become apparent and will be embarrassing. For example, if you've only worn crampons once before, tell the guide you've never worn them, as saying 'yes I've worn crampons' can mean many things. Under-promise and over-deliver is the key. For example, I went up on the Eiger North Face with a guy who told me he'd never done an alpine climb (why I took him is another matter). In reality, he'd climbed the South African route on the Central Tower of Paine!

897. Use internet forums to check out the background of any company organising a commercial trip, but remember to sift out the useful comments from those who don't understand the nature of any mountain trip, in that nothing is guaranteed (people often blame climbing companies for bad weather or poor conditions). Watch out for signs that trips are badly run – little details, such as 'bad food', 'poor-quality tents' or clients coming down with altitude problems. If in doubt, go with companies that have the biggest reputation and the most to risk, as a small independent commercial operator can often offer more of an 'exciting' trip, but that doesn't suit everyone.

898. Check what gear is included when hiring or buying into a trip, as this can increase the overall cost dramatically.

899. If you've never been on a commercial trip then steel yourself for the inevitable 'knob head' you'll have to deal with – the one person who gets on everyone's nerves. This is normal group dynamics, made more likely due to fatigue and tension, and is just part of expedition life.

900. Check the guide-to-client ratio if you want to learn anything A high-ratio course with a wide variety of experience levels tends to favour those with the most experience, and those with the least experience miss out. If in doubt, hire an instructor for a 1:1 or 1:2 course; in one day they can teach you what could take a week with a 1:8 ratio.

901. Check out cancellation policies and insurance, and, if in the UK, make sure the company is a member of the Association for Independent Tour Operators (AITO) and the Association of Bonded Travel Organisers' Trust (ABTOT) so that you're covered if they go tits up.

Speed climbing on *The Nose*, El Cap.

MAKE YOUR OWN KIT (902–913)

902. Manufacturers make kit for a broad range of consumers and very little gear is as niche as you may assume, meaning that you can always improve any item of kit by adding the things that you find missing and which the manufacturer deemed uncommercial.

903. Make your own sleeping bag – well, 'sleeping blanket' – from a kit via Ray Jardine's website (**www.rayjardine.com**). This kit allows you to build a summer-weight through to expedition-weight blanket that has many advantages over a traditional sleeping bag. First, it's synthetic, so your survivability is massively increased (down loses its insulation properties when wet, and it's slow to dry), it packs down small due to only being the top half of the bag, and it's lightweight. Even a light summer-weight bag will be warm enough for single-night winter trips when wearing all your clothes. I also like this design as it makes it much easier to move around under the blanket; taking boots off, sorting clothes etc., which is great when you're stuck in a confined space such as a bivvy tent. Ray also sells two-person blankets that are perfect for high-mountain use, saving weight and bulk, as well as sharing warmth.

904. Most bivvy bags you can buy these days don't work that well, as many manufacturers keep the price low by using non-breathable bottoms, which is a waste of time for long-term use on a mountain (basically your bag will get wet). Instead, make your own fully breathable bag using fabric from companies such as Point North (**www.profabrics.co.uk**). For alpine use where rain isn't going to be a problem, use lightweight, water-resistant Pertex Endurance top and bottom, while for big walls or places where rain is a problem, get something more heavy duty. Seal the seams with Seam Grip (you could also try iron-on seam tape), or leave them as they are for cold conditions. Make a big cowl that covers the top third of the bag, and forget about a zipper.

905. Make a gear roll; it will help you keep all your hardware in good order and in one place, and you can check it's all there at the end of the day. To do this, just buy a square metre of heavy-duty nylon (Cordura) and 2 metres of 15-millimetre tape. Sew the edges over to reinforce them, then sew the tape 20 centimetres below the top, sewing bar-tacks at 10-centimetre intervals along its length (you can thread thick plastic tubing on to this as well if you want) sewing it down with extra tacks 20 centimetres from each end. You will end up with a square of fabric with a series of clip loops along one side. Just clip in your hardware (cams, quickdraws and nuts, primarily) in a set order, so can check them in and out each time you climb. To stow, just use it like a tool roll, folding in the sides, then rolling up (you can add two straps to keep it closed, or just stow it rolled).

906. A good-quality, second-hand sewing machine (look on eBay) is the key to making good kit, especially when it comes to heavy-duty sewing. The modern, commercial sewing machines you'll find in a store will probably not be up to the job, so visit a specialist sewing machine shop and ask their advice, as they'll probably have an old machine that will do the job. Old machines tend to be built better than new ones, with metal parts that will take some punishment. Even an old-school, hand-cranked Singer machine will tackle most jobs well, and although zigzag stitches are good, a solid straight-line machine will do most things well. I use a Pfaff 130 machine, which is probably older than me, but it will sew most things (on heavy-duty fabrics, you may need to turn the wheel by hand). *(Figure 32)*

907. You can buy a lot of fabrics at a reasonable price on eBay, including heavy-duty fabrics like Cordura, meaning you can make items like stuff bags, rope bags and groundsheet protectors at a very low cost.

908. A roll of Power Stretch can make all sorts of cool items, such as wristovers and leg warmers (great for rock climbing or ice climbing). It's easy to sew, relatively cheap and robust.

909. Use heavy-duty needles for heavy-duty work – such as size 16/100 – as well as good-quality, heavy-duty bonded polyester thread (you're limited a little by a domestic machine, so don't spare the stitches).

910. Use heavy mini- and full-size paper clamps to hold heavy-duty fabrics together when sewing.

911. Make power straps for your boots out of two lengths of 25-millimetre heavy-duty polyester webbing that wraps nearly twice the circumference of the boot's ankle, two strips of Velcro that goes a little less than once around, and two Fastex square buckles. Sew the Fastex buckle on one end, then sew the two halves of Velcro on the same side of the webbing, so they meet in the middle. Wrap the strap around your ankle, thread the end of the webbing through the buckle, and finally pull tight and press the Velcro together to lock.

912. If you can't do bar tacks or zigzags, just sew a square and criss-cross the inside, double or treble sticking the top and bottom of the box.

913. The more you sew, the more you want to sew, and you'll begin seeing many bits of gear that can be improved quite easily, increasing the effectiveness of your kit.

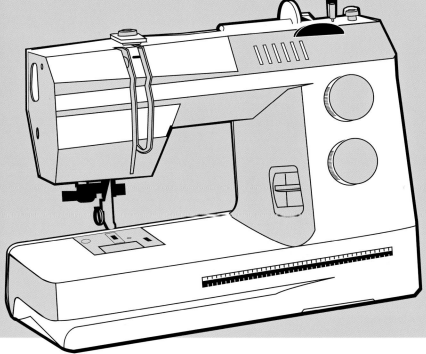

FIGURE 32

Kjersti Eide on the south ridge of Ulvetanna, Antarctica.

PHOTOGRAPHY AND VIDEO (914–952)

914. Don't forget C.H.E.W. with cameras and electronic gear … bet you want to know what that means, don't you? Well, it stands for Cold to Hot, Everything Wet (I know it's rubbish, but I just made it up). Basically, when you move something that is cold from a cold place (say sub-zero-ish) to a warm place, the moisture in the air will jump on said cold thing. With clothing you don't notice it, but with cameras, the first thing you'll see is your lens fog up. If going from super cold to room temperature, your kit will be soaked as soon as you step inside the warm room. This can be a pain and may destroy your gear (moisture may form inside the gadget and destroy it), so you need to take precautions. For a mild difference in temperature, keeping your camera or phone in a pouch and letting it gradually warm will be enough. If the difference is big (say jumping into a tent or snow hole with a stove running when it's -20 °C outside), keep the item in a dry bag or plastic bag for an hour or so to let it warm up.

915. If you're a photographer or filmmaker and want to film inside and out without all the hassle of C.H.E.W., then have two setups: one for outside that stays outside, and one for inside that is kept insulated in a pelican case inside your sleeping bag.

916. Unless you're a pro, get a small camera that you can easily carry and have it clipped to your harness in a pouch. This way your camera is always there and you will take photos, something that won't happen if it's stuck in the lid of your pack.

917. Another good way to carry a camera is in an inside chest pocket. Sew a loop inside your jacket and clip the camera to it with a lanyard so you don't drop it. To take a photo, just pull out the camera, take a shot, then stuff it away again. For this, you need a low-profile camera and I would opt for a water-resistant model so sweat doesn't damage it. Another benefit is that you don't have to worry about the camera batteries draining in the cold as you'll be keeping them warm, and the camera is not affected by C.H.E.W.

918. Attach a lanyard from your camera to your camera pouch so you can't drop it. I use a length of 4-millimetre Perlon with the core removed. I pull the camera out, take a photo, then stuff the camera and cord back in easily, with no stress about dropping it.

919. Always carry a spare battery and memory card, as batteries can quickly discharge if the camera is left on filming. And a dead battery means a dead camera.

920. Don't forget to regularly download the photos from your memory card, as cameras, no matter how well tethered, do get lost. If that happens and you haven't backed up your photos for three years, then that's a lot of lost memories.

921. If you find all your pics have been deleted by accident or the memory card has been corrupted somehow, then don't despair. There are loads of software apps out there that can rescue all those deleted files from seemingly nowhere.

922. If you're in the market for a climbing camera, always go for simple bodies that feature simple controls, and a wide-angle lens (28mm equivalent or wider).

923. Climbing cameras come in three main categories: slim compact, compact, and mini DSLR. The slim compact is just that: a thin-bodied compact camera, ideally with a fixed-focal-length wide-angle lens, that fits in the smallest camera pouches or even in a trouser pocket (or in an inside jacket pocket). Examples include the Ricoh GR or Canon PowerShot S120. The quality of these cameras varies, but the best provide awesome shots quickly and at a relatively low cost. The compact cameras are best typified by the Canon G series, a medium-size boxy compact that features far more control than a compact, including manual settings, zoom lens, and good-quality video. The mini DSLR is a step down from a full-size Nikon or Canon DSLR, having a slim body like a compact, but with the ability to swap lenses, from fixed lens to zooms. An example of a mini DSLR is the Canon 100D (Rebel SL1). Mirrorless Interchangeable Lens Cameras – such as Olympus and Panasonic Micro Four-Thirds cameras, Fuji X-Series and Nikon 1 series – are similar to the Mini DSLR in that they have interchangeable lenses, but they are smaller and lighter due to the elimination of the SLR's mirror. All are equally valid for climbing, and in the right hands any will provide a good shot. Try before you buy and see what works for you.

924. There are several very tough waterproof cameras on the market, which are small and slim, and ideal for hardcore use. The quality of the shots is not as good as some top-end compacts due to the design of a waterproof lens, but when the shit hits the fan, said pro compact would never be used.

925. Get a good variety of shots when climbing, not just bum shots of your mate. In my experience, 'nice views' are boring, and unless you happen to have a larger-format camera, you won't do them justice. Instead, try and tell the story of the climb, using pictures from both you and your partner.

926. Don't worry about getting body parts in shots, as this gives a sense of reality to the photos. Instead of high art, go for a documentary style, capturing both the good and the bad of the day.

927. The moments when you really don't want to get your camera out – the epic descent, the poor belay you fear will fail as your partner jibbers above, the enforced bivvy – are always the times when you'll get the best shots … if you find the energy to take them.

928. Talk to your partner before the climb about taking photos and make sure he or she has a camera (and it has a charged battery!).

929. A mini GorillaPod tripod weighs nothing but can be used to get some great self-timer shots on belays, or even mid-pitch. To make it suitable, lark's-foot some cord to the bottom of one leg and run this up and tie it to the head, leaving one strand left that can be tied or clipped to the camera. By clipping the 'leg cord' into a runner, you can get really effective pictures or better still video. Just make sure the whole setup is tied together, as the legs of GorillaPod tripods can come off quite easily.

930. Get a GoPro camera and play around with its time-lapse photo setting, with the camera taking photos every few seconds. If used with a mini tripod, you can get some great wide-angle shots looking down at people climbing.

931. Try to get a mix of the micro and the macro – and everything in-between – to get a sense of the climb. This means close-ups of runners, worn fingertips and lichen, right through to mountains, huge open skies and mind-bending exposure.

932. Just filming 'stuff' is very dull and leaves you with 'stuff' to edit later. Instead, get a mixture of 'stuff' and talking heads; ask your partner to 'tell us what's going on', or simply turn the camera around and film yourself. Imagine the lens is a window into your audience's world and you're showing them what's going on. This means not just talking to the camera, but talking and then showing them. This kind of thing is very effective when it comes to giving slideshows later.

933. Don't get too bogged down in the quality of video unless you're a pro. I've got shockingly poor video taken with cameras held the wrong way up, but whose subject matter (such as an avalanche bearing down) is so good that people don't even notice. Again, the bottom line is to get your camera out and film as much as possible.

934. Try to achieve a sense of scale in your photos by including people in them. One good method is to zoom in and out, taking photos. This way, when the time comes to show your photos to people, you can either ask them to spot the climber, then slowly zoom in, or do the same only backwards.

935. Look at what other climbers are doing with their photos and learn from them in order to develop your own style. I was always very influenced by war photography, so blurriness and movement always excited me, whereas someone interested in large-format prints would want something completely different.

936. Never zoom when filming, but equally don't worry too much about camera shake in your videos if it's being done in documentary style. If you're capturing the real deal, then having your camera set up on a tripod will just reduce the reality of the shots. (Check out the start of *Saving Private Ryan* or any war documentary to see what I mean.)

937. If you use a small video camera, attach some fibrepile to the internal mic to cut out wind noise, and use a lens cap attached to the body by cord. I always glue Velcro to the lens cap and have some Velcro on the side of the camera, so when I take the cap off I can just stick it out of the way. This avoids the annoying problem of the lens cap dangling in front of the lens when pointing the camera downwards.

938. Turn off digital zoom, and when hand holding your camera, try to keep the lens as wide as possible to avoid camera shake.

939. Take off the junk strap from your video camera and replace it with thin Dyneema tied with overhand knots (leave a long tail). Leave one length of tail super long and attach a karabiner to this. You now have confidence that the strap will not fail, and the karabiner can tether the camera to you.

940. Use a small SLR case designed for use with a body and a long lens to hold your video camera. This should be lower profile than a standard video bag, and placing it vertically means it is easier to carry. Again, replace the carry strap with good-quality climbing tape and don't trust plastic buckles.

FIGURE 33

941. It's an old chestnut, but the best photos are taken in the 'golden hour' (also known as the magic hour) – the hour immediately after sunrise and before sunset. Stanley Kubrick loved the golden hour so much he filmed the whole of the 'sniper' section of *Full Metal Jacket* in the evening – which is quite a slow way to make a film.

942. In snow, your camera will often get tricked by the large amount of white. Try spot focusing off a person with a mid-tone jacket, and try taking pics with a flash, even on sunny days.

943. Learn the rule of thirds and always frame your pictures well (and I'm not talking about the frames you buy from IKEA). Try to avoid placing the subject in the middle of the shot all the time, and instead have them inset in a box that takes up one third of the shot. Do some research on this, as well as the Fibonacci spiral and the golden ratio, which may sound like plot device from a Dan Brown novel, but are important aspects of all art (although they don't work well with bum shots). *(Figure 33)*

944. The most important thing about photography is light – and dark; without both you tend to end up with crap photos. The more extreme of both in the same shot, the better (think of it like hotdog and onions: you need both, otherwise it's just an onion sandwich or a mouthful of mushed-up pig's foreskin).

945. Climbing portraits are great, especially when taken before and after a trip. Ignore the rule of thirds I talked about opposite (try to only ignore 'set in stone rules' when you know better, which is never, or when someone tells you to, so you can blame them) and fill the frame with the sitter's face. This way you should get loads of details, and don't forget light and dark; have the sun shining on one side of the face.

946. If you plan on doing a lot of filming or photography then climbing as a three-person team is great, as this allows one person to film on each pitch.

947. Don't forget that the leader can take photos from above the belayer, which makes for super-effective shots.

948. Avoid doing any in-camera edits of your shots, such as making them black and white. This is best done later in photo editing software such as Photoshop or Photoshop Elements.

949. Modern DSLRs can be used for both stills and video, and there have been some very impressive little films made using a DSLR at base camp (approach shots, camp life) and with GoPros and compact cameras shooting 1080p (full HD) film on the hill. As with all climbing skills, practise before you go away, as re-shoots are not always an option!

950. If you're using an interchangeable lens camera such as a DSLR or a mirrorless camera, or you're in the market for one, focus more on the lenses and less on the bodies. New designs of bodies come along all the time, making that expensive body obsolete, but good lenses remain.

951. Choose full-frame lenses (not those designed exclusively for smaller sensors), and just pick up second-hand ones, especially old prime lenses. In my experience, one of the best lenses a climber can buy is a good-quality small 20mm lens; these are light and compact (which means you can use a small camera case), and almost everything is in focus all the time. Plus you can get shots when in cramped bivvies and belays. For a second lens, buy a small 50mm, which will work well for portraits and low light. If you want one lens to do it all, then get a lens that zooms from around 20mm to 70mm and just accept the fact that it will be heavy and bulky, meaning you won't take it out much on the hill.

952. Sound is more important than images, and story is more important than both. If you only have a great story, you can make a film with any old stills or images (other peoples' for example) and if you have good sound, it becomes easier (audio of people talking, the sound of the mountains, the rushing stream, the jingle of gear). If you have good stills and video, then you're sorted. On the other hand, good video with poor sound (a big problem with GoPro cameras) and no story …Well, no one's going to be into it as much as you.

SPONSORSHIP AND MEDIA (953–963)

953. No company is going to give gear away for nothing, no matter how amazing your trip is. You need to work out how to make it worth their while, and then back that promise up by delivery.

954. Companies want high-quality stills (hi-res, in focus and of something interesting), video and testimonials about how great their gear was (or private feedback about things that didn't work). Cheesy shots of sponsor logos on summits are OK, but what most brands want is in-your-face product placement, done in such a way that it doesn't seem overt.

955. Stay in touch with a sponsor – send emails, postcards, and offer to do a talk to the staff on your return.

956. The more you can deliver, the greater the chance the company will support you next time.

957. People often talk about writing and sending thousands of letters or emails in order to raise cash for trips, but in my experience, such people generally receive their funding in the end through a personal contact, meaning the more people in important positions you know, the better your chances are.

958. There are many grants and awards out there to apply for and most people with a good expedition plan, and who look like they can do it safely, will get something if they apply. These include: the British Mountaineering Council grants, the Mount Everest Foundation, the Nick Estcourt Award, the Winston Churchill Memorial Trust, the Alpine Club Climbing Fund grants, and many others, including in the US and European climbing communities.

959. Getting money out of companies is next to impossible. Gear is often more forthcoming, but don't take the piss. Only ask for what you really need, not what you'd like to have.

960. If you want to move up a level and work with a single company or a group of companies, then treat it as work. Be professional in all your dealing; set up a meeting and tell them directly what you need from them so they can decide if they can help. Being vague is deadly when it comes to asking for something, as you may want to ask for £500 a year, and they may think you want £50,000.

961. Tell them what support you want (call it support, as that's what it is) and show them what it's for and what you'll do in return. If it's an outdoor brand, then offer so many days of work (training, lectures, shop visits) but don't over-promise, as you may end up working for less than minimum wage. At the end of the day, if you're a talented climber, then you should be off climbing, as that will bring the most reward to everyone.

962. If you want to make some money from your trips, then writing for magazines or selling your images (ideally both) is a good way to get some return on your trip costs. The money paid in most magazines is low, but if you do a good job, they will use your stuff again and this will open doors to future kit deals, as it shows you're motivated and able to sell yourself.

963. If you want to write longer pieces, or even a book, then working up to it through writing for magazines is great training, as it both teaches you the art of writing and editing, as well as building up an audience. Without an audience, it's hard work selling books. These days the number of outlets for authors is limited and the costs involved mean that the likelihood of getting published is slim unless you're well known. Luckily, the advent of new media, such as the ebook, allows anyone to quickly produce books that can be monetised and sold globally. Setting up an Amazon account is easy and there are tons of free apps out there that can convert your Word document into an ePub ebook file.

BODILY FUNCTIONS (964–974)

964. On longer trips, try and get into the habit of going to the toilet at the same time every day, ideally when you get up. On such trips your diet tends to be pretty fixed so it's quite easy. This means once you've done toilet duties you don't have to stress about it!

965. If you're doing multi-day routes, then it's vital to get used to going to the toilet in your harness, as 'needing a crap' can really spoil your psych. Get into the habit of going before you climb.

966. Instead of a toilet roll, carry multiple small packets of tissues. One can be easily carried while climbing in case you get caught out mid-pitch.

967. If you need to have a crap in your harness and you have adjustable leg loops, then it's best to undo the leg loops and rear risers and spin the waist band 90 degrees, so the belay loop and rear risers are at your hips. This means that you won't have any 'accidents'.

968. If you don't have removable leg loops, then just undo the rear riders and pull your pants down, pulling the rear risers through your legs and clipping them off to your belay loop.

969. Try to avoid crapping where people will be walking or camping, and always do it well away from any water source. Crapping under rocks is the normal way that most people do it, but it's better to crap where the elements will break it down. You can aid this process by smearing your crap with a stick or a rock so that it breaks down faster. Otherwise bring a trowel and bury it.

970. If camping on snow for a long period you should consider packing out your crap, or disposing of it in some way, especially if it's a long expedition where the snow could melt over time. The best way to do this is to use a small blue expedition barrel lined with two heavy-duty refuse bags (and I mean heavy duty!) as a toilet. When it's almost full, shake it down to remove the bags, and either carry it out, or throw it into a crevasse.

971. If you need to have a piss, then have one, as keeping a litre of liquid at body temperature in your bladder uses up valuable calories.

972. Always carry a piss bottle and make sure it's well marked!

973. If you don't have a piss bottle, then use your mug. Just remember that the Romans routinely drank their own piss.

974. Never drink your own urine; it will taste like acid and burn your throat. If things are that bad, then you'll ignore this advice.

Welcome to Antarctica.

TRIP PACKING AND TRAVEL (975–1001)

975. If you have minimal baggage allowance, then check your bag doesn't weigh more than the kit that's in it; some bags can take up 30 per cent of your allowance even when empty.

976. Climbing gear is not considered sports equipment, like skis, golf clubs and surfboards. So get a big snowboard bag, a surfboard bag, or even a big golf bag, and fill it up to the maximum limit for sports equipment, and take this as your 'sports bag'. You will still have to pay for this on most flights, but the cost will be a fraction of what you would be charged per kilogram.

977. When packing, stuff sacks of all sizes are super handy, especially if customs officials come calling; without them, you'll end up with mountains of kit all over the floor. Mark all bags with what's in them, and people's names. Do this by sticking a patch of duct tape on the side of the bag and writing on it in marker pen.

978. If you need to adjust the weight of a team's bags, then get to the airport and weigh the bags on a free check-in desk.

979. If you're over the limit, then consider how valuable the kit you're carrying is. If you have an old tatty rope, cord or a pot of coffee, then it may be better to ditch it than pay £5 per kilogram to take it along.

980. If you're over the limit, then you can wear all your heavy clothes. Do this by making one 'super flight jacket' by layering up all your fleeces and coats. Also, you can stuff gear like batteries in your pockets.

981. Carrying a rope as hand luggage is a good way to keep the weight down, but at some airports you may be stopped by security and sent back, as it 'could be used to tie up the pilot'. If you try this, then give yourself time to go back and check it in.

982. One method of boosting your baggage allowance is to check one load in as baggage, then after leaving it a while (you'll need to get there early), go back with a second bag and tell them you've been told it has items you can't take on the plane (a rope for example) and ask to check that in as well. Most of the time, they won't have a record of the weight of your first bag and they may let you just check it in.

983. Boost your hand-luggage allowance by finding yourself the largest cheap laptop-style bag, not some slimline one for a modern laptop, but something more like a briefcase, as these can hold about 20 litres of stuff. Most flights these days allow you one bag (a 30-litre rucksack) and a second smaller under-seat computer bag, and between the two you can carry a fair amount of stuff (such smaller bags tend not to get weighed either).

984. If you're travelling to a country where gear is inexpensive, then consider buying some equipment (pans, food, stove) there in order to keep your weight down.

985. If you're taking all your own food, make sure you're allowed to bring it into the country you're travelling to, as some countries have strict rules about the import of foods.

986. When you've got a lot of stuff, including food and heavy equipment, then look into getting it shipped to your destination as it will be much cheaper. If you do this, then give yourself a few months to sort this out, as it will often be loaded on to a ship and could take a while.

987. Always travel with good-quality wax earplugs, an eye mask, and a pillow, and make sure you stay hydrated. If you know you've got a big flight that day, then get up early so you have a better chance of sleeping on the flight.

988. On long flights always try to get an aisle seat, as this means you can get up and walk around, go to the toilet, get a drink etc, rather than being 'locked in.'

989. When travelling, take a direct flight if possible and avoid a transatlantic flight followed by an internal flight, as this takes much longer and will leave you more tired than necessary at the start of your trip.

990. Jet lag can be reduced by getting some quality sleep in on the plane, and once you arrive in the destination country, avoid sleeping until everyone else is, even if it means staying awake for over twenty-four hours. If you can hold out, then once you have had one full night's sleep, you should adjust much quicker, but you'll still probably wake early for a week or so. If you do, then just get up and make the most of your day.

991. Be super careful of driving after a long journey and consider staying close to the airport if you know the flight will be a killer. It's often a good idea to be close to civilisation at the start of the trip, as you can easily buy gear you've forgotten to bring with you.

992. Always have a photocopy of your passport, birth certificate, driving licence, ticket details and the telephone number of your insurance company. Keep these in a separate place to the originals, folded up in a Ziploc bag somewhere where you have a good chance of not losing them.

993. You often see people with one of those pouches that go around the neck and which store their passport, ID and money – commonly known as a 'please mug me' pouch. No way of carrying important items is immune to theft, and if someone wants your stuff, then they will get it. Instead, try to reduce the risk of people just snatching or walking away with your valuables by having them attached, but out of the way. Money wallets are OK, but they make it look like you're hiding something, and I think low profile bumbags (flat style) that can be spun round under a jacket, work well. You can also swap a normal wallet for a Dynomighty wallet, which just looks like a piece of folded paper.

994. Try to keep petty cash separate from your wallet, cards and passport, so that you're not exposing all of your valuables each time you pay for something. Instead, carry a separate wallet that holds cash and old credit cards. You can also give this away if you get mugged, and this may let you keep your other cash.

995. Carrying spare cash, a copy of your passport and a credit card is handy if you lose all your bags and money.

996. If you have a good-quality camera or video gear, try not to look like a pro, as customs may believe you're planning on working and will want you to have a work visa.

997. Before heading off into the wild, check that all your gear has made it to your destination and it's all working. I once found out I had brought the wrong stove pump, and on another occasion I lost all the rack in a taxi.

998. Stick a coloured label on both sides of your passport with your name on it so you don't end up with the wrong passport. Make them different colours so you know what side opens out to your passport page.

999. Always have an address ready to give to immigration officers of where you plan to stay, even if it's just a campsite, and be aware that having a one-way ticket will lead to much hassling as they will think you're not going home again.

1000. Always have a pen when travelling so you can fill in your immigration form. Don't get drunk on the plane, and never joke with immigration officers.

1001. One of the most important rules of any planned climbing trip or expedition is that you're not going until the tickets are booked – and the earlier they are booked, the cheaper the trip. Until people put money down they are likely to have a change of heart, with work and other stuff getting in the way – so pay up!

Espen Fadnes keeping warm in Queen Maud Land.

Never go away without a good book!

009

READING LIST

"A selection of books which I've found to be especially useful over the years."

READING LIST

READING LIST

A selection of books which I've found to be especially useful over the years. Some are out of print, but you can usually pick them up fairly cheaply online.

Alpine Climbing by John Barry
Crowood Press, 1988.
ISBN: 1852238887
A classic text covering the basics of alpine climbing, written by one of the UK's best writers. Out of print, but you can pick up second-hand copies very cheaply online.

The Climber's Handbook by Ron Fawcett, Jeff Lowe, Paul Nunn and Alan Rouse
Sierra Club Books, 1987.
ISBN: 0871567032
A big book with a lot of interesting stuff from climbers at the top of their game. Al Rouse and Paul Nunn's alpine and expedition pages are very good. Out of print, but available second-hand.

Lightweight Expeditions by Rob Collister
Crowood Press, 1989.
ISBN: 1852231394
A great little book that's fun to read and also holds a lot of wisdom for anyone heading into the greater ranges.

Extreme Alpinism: Climbing Light, Fast, and High by Mark Twight
Mountaineers Books, 1999.
ISBN: 9780898866544
The bible for all aspiring alpinists out there.

The Complete Guide to Rope Techniques by Nigel Shepherd
Frances Lincoln, 2007 (revised edition).
ISBN: 9780711227200
Ultra classic, with simple text and every knot you need to know, plus a few you don't.

Polar Exploration: A practical handbook for North and South Pole expeditions by Dixie Dansercoer
Cicerone Press, 2012.
ISBN: 9781852846657
Even if you don't plan on heading to the poles, this book has a lot of interesting ideas on training, equipment and how to approach doing the impossible.

Pocket First Aid and Wilderness Medicine by Jim Duff and Peter Gormly
Cicerone Press, 2012.
ISBN: 1852845007
Tiny little book that really could save your life when beyond the reach of a doctor. Small enough to carry in an expedition first-aid kit, this is a book all climbers should have.

Espresso Lessons From The Rock Warrior's Way by Arno Ilgner
Desiderata Institute, 2009.
ISBN: 0974011231
A shortened version of *The Rock Warrior's Way*, full of practical advice on getting your head in gear.

Big Walls by John Long and John Middendorf
Falcon, 1994.
ISBN: 9780934641630
A classic, and although there are newer books on the market, none quite match the stories in this one.

The Dharma Bums by Jack Kerouac
Penguin Books, 1976.
ISBN: 9780140042528
Climbing would be golf without the rebellious spirit. Wildness is as much about finding ourselves as leaving behind those bizzy bodies of everyday conformity.

'Kiwi' Steve Bate on the penultimate pitch of *Zodiac*, El Cap.

about the author

The author in Queen Maud Land, Antarctica.

Climbing magazine once described **ANDY KIRKPATRICK** as a climber with a "strange penchant for the long, the cold and the difficult," with a reputation "for seeking out routes where the danger is real, and the return is questionable, pushing himself on some of the hardest walls and faces in the Alps and beyond, sometimes with partners and sometimes alone."

Beginning at the age of five, Andy learned to climb on the small gritstone outcrops of England. He quickly moved on to the walls and faces of Chamonix, and then to far flung places such as Antarctica, Patagonia, Greenland and Alaska. Although an alpine climber at heart, his first love is Yosemite's El Capitan, which he has climbed over thirty times, including five solos and two one-day ascents. His idea of heaven would be to have a free and unlimited camping permit for Tuolumne Meadows.

In 2001 he undertook an eleven-day solo ascent of the Reticent Wall on El Capitan, one of the hardest solo climbs in the world. This climb was the central theme of his first book, *Psychovertical*, which won the 2008 Boardman Tasker Prize for Mountain Literature. His second book, *Cold Wars*, won the 2012 Boardman Tasker Prize.

Andy makes his living as an award-winning writer, contrarian blogger, and stand-up comedian. His tip to life is not to be a slave to anything—to the past, to money, to popularity, to climbing—but only to love. He lives in Dublin, Ireland.

MOUNTAINEERS BOOKS is a leading publisher of mountaineering literature and guides—including our flagship title, *Mountaineering: The Freedom of the Hills*—as well as adventure narratives, natural history, and general outdoor recreation. Through our two imprints, Skipstone and Braided River, we also publish titles on sustainability and conservation. We are committed to supporting the environmental and educational goals of our organization by providing expert information on human-powered adventure, sustainable practices at home and on the trail, and preservation of wilderness.

The Mountaineers, founded in 1906, is a 501(c)(3) nonprofit outdoor activity and conservation organization whose mission is "to explore, study, preserve, and enjoy the natural beauty of the outdoors." One of the largest such organizations in the United States, it sponsors classes and year-round outdoor activities throughout the Pacific Northwest, including climbing, hiking, backcountry skiing, snowshoeing, bicycling, camping, paddling, and more. The Mountaineers also supports its mission through its publishing division, Mountaineers Books, and promotes environmental education and citizen engagement. For more information, visit The Mountaineers Program Center, 7700 Sand Point Way NE, Seattle, WA 98115-3996; phone 206-521-6001; www.mountaineers.org; or email info@mountaineers.org.

Our publications are made possible through the generosity of donors and through sales of more than 700 titles on outdoor recreation, sustainable lifestyle, and conservation. To donate, purchase books, or learn more, visit us online.

**MOUNTAINEERS
BOOKS**

1001 SW Klickitat Way, Suite 201 • Seattle, WA 98134
800-553-4453 • mbooks@mountaineersbooks.org • www.mountaineersbooks.org

YOU MIGHT ALSO ENJOY THESE TITLES

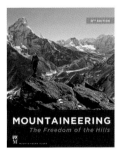